大学
实用英语综合教程
练习册（一）

主　编　周晓红　　陈丽琴　　谢胜平
副主编　郑慧静　　余晓春　　朱　琳

北京理工大学出版社
BEIJING INSTITUTE OF TECHNOLOGY PRESS

版权专有　侵权必究

图书在版编目（CIP）数据

大学实用英语综合教程练习册.1/周晓红，陈丽琴，谢胜平主编.—北京：北京理工大学出版社，2012.8（2017.9重印）
ISBN 978-7-5640-6723-6

Ⅰ.①大…　Ⅱ.①周…②陈…③谢…　Ⅲ.①英语-高等学校-习题集　Ⅳ.①H319.6

中国版本图书馆CIP数据核字（2012）第196685号

出版发行 /	北京理工大学出版社
社　　址 /	北京市海淀区中关村南大街5号
邮　　编 /	100081
电　　话 /	（010）68914775（办公室）68944990（批销中心）68911084（读者服务部）
网　　址 /	http://www.bitpress.com.cn
经　　销 /	全国各地新华书店
印　　刷 /	三河市华骏印务包装有限公司
开　　本 /	787毫米×1092毫米　1/16
印　　张 /	10
字　　数 /	210千字
版　　次 /	2012年8月第1版　2017年9月第7次印刷
定　　价 /	24.80元

责任校对 / 周瑞红
责任印制 / 王美丽

图书出现印装质量问题，本社负责调换

编 委 会

（按姓氏笔画排名）

万传花	万妮娜	文　玲	邓胜平	邓　睿	叶　韡	华　美
刘洪清	刘美丽	刘　敏	刘　婷	朱　琳	陈丽琴	陈　茜
陈　娟	何　玉	何　婷	李　沛	李晓霞	李海娇	李　聊
邱黄辉	邱敏华	邱银兰	苏　焕	汪小莉	肖志华	肖　珠
余晓春	张象成	罗海琳	罗湘娜	宗也萍	周晓红	郑慧静
段园园	胡若冰	姜　懿	赵　静	贺　敏	高　萍	袁志芸
袁　超	黄　丽	彭明蓉	谢胜平	曾雅静	蔡琮瑶	

Preface 前言

《大学实用英语综合教程练习册》共分3册,每册都以教程相对应的课文翻译、练习及练习答案的形式表现,内容新颖实用、条理清晰、通俗易懂、针对性强。《大学实用英语综合教程练习册(一)》为第一册,第一部分为教程课文的翻译与练习的解答,第二部分为模拟试题与真题汇编,第三部分为参考答案与详细解析。在每单元里围绕一个主题,分别对教程里的课文进行标准的翻译,对课后的练习进行详细的解答,每单元还配以选择题、小阅读的题型,并附有参考答案。

本套系列教材及配套习题吸取了现行国内外同类教材的优点,以我国高职高专人才培养特点和教学改革的最新成果为依据,突出教学内容的实用性和针对性,将语言基础能力与实际涉外交际能力的培养有机地结合起来,以满足21世纪全球化社会经济发展对高职高专人才的要求。

《大学实用英语综合教程练习册(一)》由周晓红、陈丽琴、谢胜平担任主编,郑慧静、余晓春、朱琳担任副主编。

本书在编写过程中参阅了大量的国内外相关资料和文献,得到了来自各界同人的鼓励、支持和关注,在此谨向他们表示感谢,并向有关机构、作者和资料的提供者致以诚挚的谢意。

由于编写时间仓促,书中不当之处在所难免,敬请广大同行专家和读者批评指正。

编 者

Contents 目录

Unit 1　College Life　/ 1

Part One　Listening Practice　/ 1
Part Two　Detailed Reading　/ 2
Part Three　Exercises　/ 2
Part Four　Supplementary Reading　/ 3

Unit 2　Books　/ 19

Part One　Listening Practice　/ 19
Part Two　Detailed Reading　/ 20
Part Three　Exercises　/ 21
Part Four　Supplementary Reading　/ 22

Unit 3　Generation　/ 36

Part One　Listening Practice　/ 36
Part Two　Detailed Reading　/ 37
Part Three　Exercises　/ 38
Part Four　Supplementary Reading　/ 39

Unit 4　Friendship　/ 55

Part One　Listening Practice　/ 55
Part Two　Detailed Reading　/ 56
Part Three　Exercises　/ 57
Part Four　Supplementary Reading　/ 58

Unit 5　Romance　/ 75

Part One　Listening Practice　/ 75
Part Two　Detailed Reading　/ 76
Part Three　Exercises　/ 77
Part Four　Supplementary Reading　/ 78

Unit 6　Money　/ 92

Part One　Listening Practice　/ 92
Part Two　Detailed Reading　/ 93
Part Three　Exercises　/ 94
Part Four　Supplementary Reading　/ 95

Unit 7　Internet　/ 110

Part One　Listening Practice　/ 110
Part Two　Detailed Reading　/ 111
Part Three　Exercises　/ 112
Part Four　Supplementary Reading　/ 113

Unit 8　Entertainment　/ 126

Part One　Listening Practice　/ 126
Part Two　Detailed Reading　/ 127
Part Three　Exercises　/ 128
Part Four　Supplementary Reading　/ 129

Unit 1

College Life

Part One Listening Practice

Section A

1. A   2. A   3. A   4. A   5. B
6. B   7. A   8. A   9. B   10. A
11. A   12. A   13. B   14. A   15. B
16. B   17. A   18. B   19. B   20. B

Section B

Task 1

1) How about you   2) in fact   3) By the way
4) in our university

Task 2

5) colder and colder   6) Nice to meet   7) new
8) a new intern   9) small world   10) same company
11) as an accountant   12) sales department

Part Two Detailed Reading

家庭教育和学校教育

　　一项研究表明，目前，家庭和学校的关系不太和谐。一些学校声称家长给了孩子过多的关心和爱护，这让孩子很容易变得以自我为中心；而家长则抱怨，学校让孩子紧张并引发他们的焦虑情绪。

　　家庭教育有其自身的优点与不足。父母的言行会影响孩子的世界观。而且，在家庭中让孩子学会如何感受别人的爱并给予回报是非常重要的。但是，家庭成员能教给孩子的东西毕竟有限。孩子在家庭中能得到内心情绪的满足，却学不到什么有用的技能。所以，尽管家庭教育对孩子的成长非常重要，可要为孩子创造光明的未来，仅仅有家庭教育是远远不够的。

　　跟家庭教育相比，学校教育看起来更为必要和实用。首先，学生能学到尽可能多的不同领域的知识。学校的图书馆和讲座能提供很多可用的资源，这些资源会向学生传递足够的信息。其次，学校就像一个社会，不同性格的人在这里一起生活，学生能从这个大环境中受益，塑造良好的、积极的、独立的个性。再次，学校里各类的组织和活动会帮助学生学习如何与不同类型的人沟通交流，如何自己处理问题。但是，学校教育也有缺点，比如不合理的教学系统和设置不科学的考试。

　　总之，家庭教育和学校教育在学生的生活中都扮演着重要的角色。但是两者都并不完美。因此，家庭和学校应该紧密合作，为了孩子的健康成长和美好未来，家庭和学校应该各自取长补短。

Comprehension of the Text

1. B　　　2. A　　　3. C　　　4. A　　　5. D

Part Three Exercises

Task 1

1. f　　　2. i　　　3. h　　　4. g　　　5. a

Unit 1

6. e 7. j 8. d 9. b 10. c

Task 2

1. explore   2. unique   3. annual   4. must   5. religious
6. session   7. stressful 8. shortcuts 9. Applicants 10. community

Task 3

1. It happened prior to my arrival.
2. Let's keep in touch.
3. Our college enrolled 1,000 new students this year.
4. As the wages were low, there were few applicants for the job.
5. Prices vary with the seasons.

Task 4

(omitted)

Part Four Supplementary Reading

译文

如何选专业？

面对数百个专业、数千所学校的选择，学生们该如何决定学什么专业和去哪儿上学呢？对一些学生来说，首先就是决定专业。

有的学生对某个项目充满热情；有的学生在高中时就有自己擅长的领域；有的学生有职业规划，比如想做护士、教师、艺术家或者工程师，这些都可以帮助他们决定自己所要学的专业。但是大部分学生对此茫然无知。

大部分老师都一致认为在选择专业时，学生需要考虑他们喜欢做什么，有哪些特殊技能以及乐于学习的程度。为有助于学生选择专业，各所大学都会提供最好的资源。许多学校都会在自家的网站上张贴大量的信息，并提供很多工具以帮助候选的和在校的学生选择专业。最常被人引用的建议包括以下几点：

深入认识自己。 学术强项和弱项是什么？兴趣是什么？价值观是什么？毕业后的目标是什么？——是工作还是读研？

做个性或者兴趣测试。 要是在中学或城镇没有这类测试的话，学生可以在自己国家的美国教育咨询与信息中心找得到。

登录大学各院系的网站。 查找列出的专业、研究相关课程与毕业要求。有些老师会在其学校的网站上公布他们的课程要求，全面描述课程概况。学生对一个专业相关的各项课程与作业要求了解得越详细越好。

到美国后，可走访一些学校的院系办公室。 可以与教职员和学生交流，也可以去学校就业中心查找就业报告，因为报告列出了新毕业生的就业情况以及他们毕业的专业。

注册后，在不同的院系试听课程。 了解开课的教师及选择听他们课的学生状况。

要是觉得自己选错了专业，也不必太担心。在美国大学里学生换专业的现象非常普遍。最好不要选择自己不喜欢或者认为没有挑战性和学习动力的专业。

不要将专业选择与职业选择混同。 任何一个专业都可以锻炼学生以胜任将来很多不同的工作岗位。正如华盛顿州立大学在其网站上所宣称的"大学教育为你进入人才市场做准备，而不限制你的职业选择"。

Comprehension of the Text

1. They should consider what they like to do, what their abilities are, and how they like to learn.
2. They can change their majors.
3. Any major can prepare students for a number of different job possibilities, so choosing a major does not mean choosing a career.

自我测试题

第一部分 单项填空

从 [A]、[B]、[C]、[D] 四个选项中，选出可以填入空白处的最佳选项，并在答题卡上将该项涂黑。

Example：
It is generally considered unwise to give a child _____ he or she wants.

[A] however [B] whatever [C] whichever [D] whenever

Answer： [A] [■] [C] [D]

---

1. —Why did you leave that position?
   —I _____ a better position at IBM.
   [A] offer [B] offered [C] am offered [D] was offered

2. The smog is due _____ invisible gases, mostly from automobile exhaust.
   [A] from   [B] to   [C] for   [D] with
3. He never said that he was good at mathematics, _____?
   [A] was he   [B] wasn't he   [C] did he   [D] didn't he
4. Danby left words with my secretary _____ he would call again in the afternoon.
   [A] who   [B] that   [C] as   [D] which
5. As it's known to everyone, _____ you work very hard, you won't pass the English final test.
   [A] unless   [B] whenever   [C] although   [D] if
6. Li Ming _____ a book about applying for universities in the United States and now he must have finished it.
   [A] has written   [B] wrote   [C] had written   [D] was writing
7. You are only allowed to do _____ you have been told to do.
   [A] how   [B] after   [C] what   [D] when
8. Tom managed to finish his university education, _____ his family was very poor.
   [A] ever since   [B] now that   [C] even though   [D] even as
9. Since Linda played a role in that film, our telephone hasn't stopped ringing. People _____ to ask what her next film is.
   [A] phone   [B] will phone   [C] were phoning [D] are phoning
10. It is what you do rather than what you say _____ matters.
    [A] that   [B] what   [C] which   [D] this
11. —What about this one?
    —Yes, it _____ very soft. Can I try it on?
    [A] is feeling   [B] felt   [C] feels   [D] is felt
12. _____ the numbers in employment, the hotel industry was the second largest industry in this country last year.
    [A] In line with [B] In terms of   [C] In accordance with [D] In proportion to
13. Li Ming, look at yourself. _____ you go to a wedding in such a suit?
    [A] Must   [B] Can   [C] May   [D] Need
14. The president said that he would cancel the visit, _____ that he was waiting for a better time.
    [A] having added [B] to add   [C] adding   [D] added
15. As we joined the big crowd, I got _____ from my friends.
    [A] separated   [B] spared   [C] lost   [D] missed

第二部分 完形填空

阅读下面短文,从短文后所给的四个选项([A]、[B]、[C]、[D])中选出能填入相应空白处的最佳选项,并在答题卡上将该项涂黑。

The report came to the British on May 21, 1941. The German battleship Bismarck, the most __16__ warship in the world, was moving out into the Atlantic Ocean. Her task was to destroy the ships __17__ supplies from the United States to war-torn England.

The British __18__ such a task. No warship they had could __19__ the Bismarck in __20__ or in firepower. The Bismarck had eight 15-inch guns and 81 smaller guns. She could move at 30 nautical mile (海里) an hour. She was believed to be unsinkable. However, the British had to __21__ her. They sent out a task force __22__ by their best battleship Hood to hunt down the Bismarck. On May 24, the Hood found the Bismarck.

It was a __23__ that the German commander (指挥官) did not want to see. His orders were __24__ the British ships that were carrying __25__, but to stay away from a fight with British warships.

The battle didn't last long. The Bismarck's first torpedo (鱼雷) __26__ the Hood, which went down taking all but three of her 1,419 men with her.

But in the __27__, the Bismarck was slightly damaged. Her commander decided to run for repairs __28__ France, which had __29__ been taken by the Germans. The British force __30__ her. __31__, because of the Bismarck's speed and the __32__ fog, they lost __33__ of her.

For two days, every British ship in the Atlantic __34__ find the Bismarck, but with no success. Finally, she was sighted by a plane from Ireland. Trying to slow the Bismarck __35__ so that their ships could catch up with her, the British fired at her from the air. The Bismarck was hit.

On the morning of May 27, the last battle was fought. Four British ships fired on the Bismarck, and she was finally sunk.

16. [A] powerful [B] long [C] quick [D] heavy
17. [A] carried [B] to carry [C] carrying [D] carry
18. [A] had feared [B] fearing [C] feared [D] have feared
19. [A] hit [B] beat [C] destroy [D] match
20. [A] weight [B] speed [C] length [D] sea
21. [A] meet [B] avoid [C] sink [D] fight with
22. [A] organized [B] supported [C] sent [D] headed
23. [A] meeting [B] conference [C] ship [D] day
24. [A] to destroy [B] to rob [C] to watch [D] to fight with
25. [A] soldiers [B] supplies [C] gun [D] planes
26. [A] sunk [B] hit [C] destroyed [D] missed
27. [A] end [B] sea [C] fight [D] day
28. [A] from [B] at [C] to [D] in
29. [A] at times [B] sometimes [C] at that time [D] all the time
30. [A] found [B] followed [C] watched [D] saw
31. [A] Although [B] But [C] Therefore [D] However
32. [A] white [B] big [C] large [D] heavy

33. [A] control [B] sight [C] faith [D] contact
34. [A] couldn't [B] managed to [C] was unable to [D] tried to
35. [A] down [B] out [C] up [D] off

第三部分 阅 读 理 解

阅读下列短文，从每题所给的四个选项（[A]、[B]、[C]、[D]）中选出最佳选项，并在答题卡上将该项涂黑。

A

The World Health Organization now supports the use of DDT in homes to control malaria. The agency supported indoor spraying with DDT and other insect poisons until the early 1980s. It stopped as health and environmental concerns about DDT increased.

But last Friday, an assistant director-general of the United Nations agency announced a policy change. Anarfi Asamoa-Baah said indoor spraying is useful to quickly reduce the number of infections caused by malaria-carrying mosquitoes. Doctor Asamoa-Baah said DDT presents no health risk when used correctly.

The W.H.O. says it supports indoor spraying in areas with high malaria rates, including throughout Africa. But its malaria program director, Arata Kochi, says DDT should be used only inside houses and huts, not outside and not for agriculture use.

In the 1940s, was found to be an excellent way to control insects. It cost little to produce and was not found to harm humans. So it was widely used for people and crops.

But in the 1960s, environmentalist Rachel Carson and her book *Silent Spring* led to a movement to ban it. The United States did just that in the 1970s.

Rachel Carson warned that DDT stayed in the environment for many years. She also warned that it thinned the shells of unborn birds and caused health problems for other animals.

Yet the rise of malaria has led some environmental groups to change their thinking. The group Environmental Defense, which led the anti-DDT movement, now supports indoor use to control malaria.

The W.H.O. says malaria sickens five hundred million people and results in more than one million deaths every year. Each day, an estimated three thousand babies and young children die from it. The large majority of deaths are in Africa, south of the Sahara.

But many critics of DDT worry it will not be used with great care. University of Illinois scientist May Berenbaum argues that DDT is not as effective as people might think. Writing in *The Washington Post*, she noted that some African mosquitoes developed resistance to it. She says DDT should be only one tool among many for insect control.

The W.H.O. supports other interventions as well. But it says India sharply cut malaria rates in the past with indoor use of DDT. And ten countries in southern Africa are currently using it for malaria control.

36. When did Americans stop using DDT?

[A] In the 1940s. [B] In the 1960s.

[C] In the 1970s. [D] In the 1980s.

37. What do you think the book "*Silent Spring*" is about?

[A] About the harm DDT does to humans.

[B] About DDT in the water from a spring.

[C] About DDT in the water used for controlling insects.

[D] About DDT used for people and crops.

38. Which of the following is NOT true?

[A] DDT may be harmful when used incorrectly.

[B] The Environmental Defense admits DDT can control malaria.

[C] DDT may be harmful to the environment and crops.

[D] All scientists agree to spray DDT indoors now.

39. What does the word "It" in the last sentence of para. I refer to?

[A] "The use of DDT." [B] "Mosquito."

[C] "The W. H. O." [D] "Malaria."

40. What can you infer from the passage?

[A] People's knowledge of a thing is always developing.

[B] DDT is very useful.

[C] There are many tools to control malaria.

[D] India has never stopped using DDT.

B

Everyone becomes a little more forgetful as they get older, but men's minds decline more than women's, according to the results of a worldwide survey.

Certain differences seem to be inherent in male and female brains: Men are better at maintaining and dealing with mental images (useful in mathematical reasoning and spatial skills), while women tend to excel (擅长) at recalling information from their brain's files (helpful with language skills and remembering the locations of objects).

Many studies have looked for a connection between sex and the amount of mental decline (衰退) people experience as they age, but the results have been mixed.

Some studies found more age-related decline in men than in women, while others saw the opposite or even no relationship at all between sex and mental decline. Those results could be improper because the studies involved older people, and women live longer than men: The men tested are the survivors, "So they're the ones that may not have shown such cognitive decline," said study team leader Elizabeth of the University of Warwick in England.

People surveyed completed four tasks that tested sex-related cognitive skills: matching an object to its rotated form, matching lines shown from the same angle, typing as many words in a particular category (范畴) as possible in the given time, e.g. "object usually colored gray," and recalling the location of objects in a line drawing. The first two were tasks at which men usually excel; the latter are typically dominated by women.

Within each age group studied, men and women performed better in their separate categories on average. And though performance declined with age for both genders, women showed obviously less decline than men overall.

41. The underlined word in the second paragraph means _____.
    [A] natural   [B] great   [C] obvious   [D] absolute
42. According to the passage, which of the following can NOT be typed into the same category?
    [A] Cloud.   [B] Sheep.   [C] Trees.   [D] Goose.
43. Which of the following statements is true according to the article?
    [A] Men do better than women when it comes to learning English.
    [B] Women stand out at remembering people's names.
    [C] Men excel at typing as many words in a particular category as possible in the given time.
    [D] Women excel at dealing with mathematic problems.
44. One important factor that affects the correctness of the results is that _____.
    [A] the old men tested may not have shown such cognitive decline
    [B] people surveyed are all old
    [C] people taking part in this test came from all over the world
    [D] women live longer than men
45. The author aims to tell us that _____.
    [A] women's minds perform better than men's
    [B] men's minds decline more with age
    [C] everyone becomes a little more forgetful as they get older
    [D] a survey on human's mind decline was done recently

C

I love charity shops and so do lots of other people in Britain because you find quite a few of them on every high street. The charity shop is a British institution, selling everything from clothes to electric goods, all at very good prices. You can get things you won't find in the shops anymore. The thing I like best about them is that your money is going to a good cause and not into the pockets of profit-driven companies, and you are not damaging the planet, but finding a new home for unwanted goods.

The first charity shop was opened in 1947 by Oxfam. The famous charity's appeal to aid postwar Greece had been so successful that it had been flooded with donations (捐赠物). They decided to set up a shop to sell some of these donations to raise money for that appeal. Now there are over 7,000 charity shops in the UK. My favorite charity shop in my hometown is the Red Cross shop, where I always find children's books, all 10 or 20 pence each.

Most of the people working in the charity shops are volunteers, although there is often a manager who gets paid. Over 90% of the goods in the charity shops are donated by the public.

Every morning you see bags of unwanted items outside the front of shops, although they don't encourage this, rather ask people to bring things in when the shop is open.

The shops have very low running costs: all profits go to charity work. Charity shops raise more than £110 million a year, funding medical research, overseas aid, supporting sick and poor children, homeless and disabled people, and much more. What better place to spend your money? You get something special for a very good price and a good moral sense. You provide funds to a good cause and tread lightly on the environment.

46. The author loves the charity shop mainly because of _____.
    [A] its convenient location   [B] its great variety of goods
    [C] its spirit of goodwill   [D] its nice shopping environment
47. The first charity shop in the UK was set up to _____.
    [A] sell cheap products   [B] deal with unwanted things
    [C] raise money for patients   [D] help a foreign country
48. Which of the following is TRUE about charity shops?
    [A] The operating costs are very low. [B] The staff are usually well paid.
    [C] 90% of the donations are second-hand. [D] They are open twenty-four hours a day.
49. Which of the following may be the best title for the passage?
    [A] What to Buy at Charity Shops
    [B] Charity Shop: Its Origin & Development
    [C] Charity Shop: Where You Buy to Donate
    [D] The Public's Concern about Charity Shops

D

My parents were in a huge argument, and I was really upset about it. I didn't know who I should talk with about how I was feeling. So I asked Mom to allow me to stay the night at my best friend's house. Though I knew I wouldn't tell her about my parents' situation, I was looking forward to getting out of the house. I was in the middle of packing up my things when suddenly the power went out in the neighborhood. Mom came to tell me that I should stay with my grandpa until the power came back on.

I was really disappointed because I felt that we did not have much to talk about. But I knew he would be frightened alone in the dark. I went to his room and told him that I'd stay with him until the power was restored. He was quite happy and said, "Great opportunity."

"What is?" I asked.

"To talk, you and I," he said, "To hold a private little meeting about what we're going to do with your mom and dad, and what we're going to do with ourselves now that we're in the situation we are in."

"But we can't do anything about it, Grandpa." I said, surprised that here was someone with whom I could share my feelings and someone who was in the same "boat" as I was.

And that's how the most unbelievable friendship between my grandfather and me started.

Sitting there in the dark, we talked about our feelings and fears of life — from how fast things change to how they sometimes don't change fast enough. That night, because the power went out, I found a new friend, with whom I could safely talk about all my fears and pains, whatever they may be.

Suddenly, the lights all came back on. "Well," he said, "I guess that means you'll want to go now. I really like our talk. I hope the power will go out every few nights!"

50. I wished to get out of the house because _____.
    [A] I was angry about my parents' quarrel
    [B] I found nobody to share my feelings with
    [C] I wanted to escape from the dark house
    [D] I planned to tell my friend about my trouble

51. Grandpa was happy to see me because _____.
    [A] he could discuss the problem with me   [B] he had not seen me for a long time
    [C] he was afraid of darkness   [D] he felt quite lonely

52. What can be inferred from the passage?
    [A] The grandchild was eager to leave.   [B] They would have more chats.
    [C] The lights would go out again.   [D] It would no longer be dark.

E

Once the 2008 Olympic Games finishes, the drums and trumpets (喇叭) of the competitions would also stop. But would the city remain as lively as it would be after this world event? Investment sustainability and high demand are two highly invaluable economic concepts (概念) that can be looked at in order to ensure post-Olympics flourish, or perhaps, an even better future for Beijingers.

Naturally, an economic downturn occurs in an Olympic host city once the major event finishes. Renmin University Professor Jin Yuanpu noted that a global event like this would put Beijing into a position of large importance in the international stage. But after this event, who would use the heavily-funded equipment and public and private investments left in the city? Various economists argued that a meltdown (彻底垮台) is highly unlikely. Jonathan Anderson, UBS Asia economist, suggested that the negative effects of the end of Beijing Olympics 2008 on the entire country aren't important compared to previous host cities. China is such a huge economy that the conclusion of the Olympics Games is the same as an ant-bite on a dragon.

But what about post-Olympics Beijing? Retired Headmaster of Peking University, Li Yining, noted that a long-term civil demand growth and a popular desire by companies to adopt careful financial management decisions can lead to continued investment growth. Even though demand in some departments of the economy would drop in the short-run, creativity, practicality and innovation would be the key factors that would continually enhance the city's image and flourish long after the Olympics in the city has ended.

So what's next for Beijing after the Olympics? Well, it's business as usual...

53. Which of the following is the author's idea?

   [A] Beijing's economy will have a downturn after the 2008 Olympic Games.

   [B] The 2008 Olympic Games have no effects on Beijing's economy.

   [C] Beijing's economy will go on as usual.

   [D] Beijing's economy will go worse after the 2008 Olympic Games.

54. Why did Jonathan Anderson believe that the negative effects of the end of Beijing Olympics 2008 on the entire country aren't important?

   [A] The negative effects are small.

   [B] The Chinese government has many measures to take.

   [C] The Chinese economy has developed at a certain level so that the negative effects can't affect it too much.

   [D] Jonathan Anderson liked China very much so he didn't want China to go worse.

55. Choose the best title for this passage.

   [A] Beijing After the Olympics

   [B] The Negative Effects of the End of Beijing Olympics

   [C] Can Beijing Get Through the Difficult Period After the 2008 Olympic Games

   [D] Beijing's Economy After the 2008 Olympic Games

第四部分　写　作

第一节　短文改错

此题要求改正所给短文中的错误。对标有题号的每一行做出判断：如无错误，在该行右边横线上画一个勾（√）；如有错误（每行只有一个错误），则按下列情况改正：

此行多一个词：把多余的词用斜线（＼）划掉，在该行右边横线上写出该词，并也用斜线划掉。

此行缺一个词：在缺词处加一个漏字符号（∧），在该行右边横线上写出该加的词。

此行错一个词：在错的词下画一横线，在该行右边横线上写出改正后的词。

注意：原行没有错的不要改。

A language is always changed. In a society	56. _____
which life continues year after year without obvious changes,	57. _____
even the change doesn't change much, too. The earliest known	58. _____
languages have difficult grammar but a small limit vocabulary.	59. _____
Over the centuries, the grammar changed and the vocabulary grown.	60. _____
For an example, the English and Spanish who	61. _____
came to America during the 16th and the 17th century	62. _____
gave the name to all the plants and animals.	63. _____
In this way, hundreds new words and expressions	64. _____
and idioms introduced into English and Spanish vocabularies.	65. _____

第二节　书面表达

假定你是李明，是一名中学生，你对部分同学沉迷于玩电子游戏（video games）的现象很着急，便向一家英文报社编辑部寄了一封信，阐述了玩电子游戏的坏处并表达了自己对这种现象的看法。

要点如下：

1. 电子游戏的普遍流行；
2. 同学们的痴迷程度；
3. 电子游戏带来的不良影响；
4. 自己的建议。

参考词汇如下：

电子游戏：video games

逃学：play truant

注意：词数 100 个左右。

参考答案及解析

第一部分　单项填空

1. D【解析】offer 在这里意为"提供"，常用结构是"主语+offer+直接宾语+间接宾语"。这里的意思是"别人"为"我"提供了一份在 IBM 的工作，所以"我"是 offer 的受动者（相当于前述结构中的间接宾语），在这里就要用被动语态。此外，从问句中可知此处时态应该用一般过去时，故选 D。

2. B【解析】due to 是一个固定搭配，表示原因。

3. C【解析】附加疑问句的构成原则是"前肯后否，前否后肯，人称、时态一致"。本句中主干部分用的是一般过去时的否定形式，所以附加部分应该用 did he，故选 C。

4. B【解析】he would call again in the afternoon 是 words 的同位语，一般要用 that 引导同位语从句，故选 B。

5. A【解析】unless 意为"除非，如果不"，whenever 意为"无论何时"，although 意为"虽然，尽管"，if 意为"如果"。本题的意思是"众所周知，除非努力学习，否则你是不能通过英语期末考试的"。因此，我们应该用 unless 作连接词。

6. D【解析】说话人推测李明的书该写完了，可知写书这一动作是过去发生的，首先就可以排除选项 A。由于写书是一段时间的事情，所以应该用过去进行时，故选 D。

7. C【解析】宾语从句中缺少一个动词宾语，而四个选项中只有 what 能作宾语，故选 C。

8. C【解析】ever since 意为"从那时到现在"，now that 意为"既然"，even though 意为"即使"，even as 意为"正巧在……的时候，正如"。本句的意思是"虽然他家境贫寒，Tom 还是完成了大学教育"。因此，填入空白处的最佳答案是 even though。

9. D【解析】题干中第二句里的宾语从句用的是一般现在时，所以主句不能用过去的时态，因此因为可以排除 C 项。由第一句话"自从 Linda 在那部电影里饰演了一个角色之后，我们的电话就响个不停"，可知人们是在不停地打电话，应该用进行时态。剩下的三个选项中只有 D 项用的是现在进行时，故选 D。

10. A【解析】本题考查强调句的用法。what you do rather than what you say 为强调部分。强调句结构为"it is（was）+被强调部分+that（who）+句子其他部分"，故选 A。

11. C【解析】feel 在这里作系动词，与 be 的用法相似，不用于被动语态和进行时态，再加上这里要用一般现在时，所以填入文中空白处的正确形式是 feels。

12. B【解析】in line with 意为"符合"，in terms of 意为"在……方面，根据"，in accordance with 意为"与……一致，依照"，in proportion to 意为"与……成比例"。本句的意思是"按员工数量计算，在去年餐饮业是这个国家的第二大行业。"故选 B。

13. B【解析】must 意为"必须"，can 意为"能够，可以"，may 意为"可以，也许，可能"，need 意为"必要，必须"。从句意来推测，李明应该是穿着不整洁，因而说话人问他"你能穿这样的衣服去参加婚礼吗？"，应该用 can 这个词。

14. C【解析】若用 having added，则表示 add 这一动作在 say 之前发生，而两者实际上是同时发生或 add 紧接 say 后发生。因此，我们可以排除 A 项。to add 表示目的，而这里是伴随的意思，所以 B 也不正确。added 有被动的意思，而这里总统是 add 这个动作的发出者，所以 D 也不正确。adding 可用在这里做伴随状语，故选 C。

15. A【解析】separate 意为"分开，隔开"，spare 意为"节约，节省，不伤害"，lose 意为"失去，丧失，错过"，miss 意为"错过，未得到，未达到"。本题的意思是"当我们混进人群的时候，我就和朋友们分开了"。因此，应该用 separate。

第二部分　完形填空

16. A【解析】long，heavy 和 quick 的最高级都是由词尾加 -est 构成，因此可以很容易地排除这三个选项。powerful 意为"强大的"。Bismarck 战舰是德国在第二次世界大战期间建造的，凭借其航速和火力系统方面的表现而号称当时最强大的战舰。

17. C【解析】本题考查非谓语动词的用法。carried 是过去分词，含有被动的意思。to carry 是动词不定式，含有"将来发生"的意思，或表示目的。carrying 是动词-ing 形式，含有主动的意思。由于 ship 是 carry 的动作发出者，所以 carried 不正确。Bismarck 战舰要袭击的是载着补给的船只，而不是准备装载补给的船只，因此 carrying 比 to carry 更为合适。

18. A【解析】本题需要选择一个充当谓语的动词，因此选项 B 首先被排除。本文讲述的是第二次世界大战期间的事，选项 D 用的是现在完成时，也可被排除。如果使用 feared，那么句子的意思就是"英国人对这一任务感到恐惧"；如果使用 had feared，那么句子的意思是"英国人早就害怕这种任务"。在战争这样严肃的环境中，英国人应该一开始就担心补给舰队被德国海军袭击，而不是出现这种危险时才感到害怕。因此，使用 had feared 更为合理。

19. D【解析】hit 意为"打出，碰撞"，beat 意为"敲打，打败"，destroy 意为"破坏，消灭"，match 意为"相比，匹配"。这里作者是在将俄罗斯战舰的航速和火力方面与其他战舰进行比较，因此，本题的正确选项是 D。

20. B【解析】weight 意为"重量"，speed 意为"速度"，length 意为"长度"。后面介绍了 Bismarck 战舰载有 8 门 15 英寸①的大炮和 81 门其他小炮，这是对其"火力"进行描述；

---

① 1 英寸=2.54 厘米。

接着作者又提到 Bismarck 战舰每小时航速可达 30 海里①，这是对其"速度"进行描述。因此，这里应该选择 speed 以实现文章前后相应。

21. C【解析】meet 意为"遇见，迎接"，avoid 意为"避免，消除"，sink 意为"使……下沉"，fight with 意为"与……战斗"。从文章的意思来看，英国人必须迎战 Bismarck 战舰，因此选项 B 可以被排除。剩下的三个选项放回原处，意思均正确，语法也没有错误。这样的题是完形填空中最难做出正确选择的。考生这时要明确一点：完形填空是选择最佳选项，而不仅仅是选择正确选项。本句前面的一句话"She was believed to be unsinkable."中的 unsinkable 一词意为"不可沉没的"，由动词 sink 演变而来。因此，为了保持文章的连贯性，sink 是本题的最佳选项。

22. D【解析】organize 意为"组织"，support 意为"支持，支援"，send 意为"派遣"，head 意为"作为……的首领"。一般每支舰队都有一艘旗舰，这支旗舰通常是舰队里最强大的，承担舰队的指挥工作。本题的意思是让 Hood 号战舰率领这支舰队。因此，正确的选项是 D。

23. A【解析】meeting 意为"会战，会见"，conference 意为"会议"，ship 意为"船只"，day 意为"日子"。A、C 和 D 放回原文中都能使句意完整、合理，但由于英国舰队不止有一艘船，而文章又没有强调战斗的日子，因此，本题的最佳选项是 A。

24. A【解析】to destroy 意为"摧毁"，to rob 意为"抢夺，抢掠"，to watch 意为"监视"，to fight with 意为"与……战斗"。文章第一段明确提出了 Bismarck 战舰的任务："Her task was to destroy the ships carrying supplies…"德国人的任务是摧毁运送补给的船只，而并非抢夺、监视或是与其战斗。因此，本题的正确答案是 A。

25. B【解析】本题仍然从"Her task was to destroy the ships carrying supplies…"处可以得出答案。

26. B【解析】sink 意为"击沉"，hit 意为"击中"，destroy 意为"击毁"，miss 意为"未击中"。从后面英军的损失来看，鱼雷击中了 Hood 号，但未造成严重伤害。因此，正确选项是 B。

27. C【解析】in the end 意为"最后"，in the sea 意为"在海里"，in the fight 意为"在战斗中"，in the day 意为"在一天内"。本句要表达的是"Bismarck 战舰在战斗中受了轻伤"，因此，本题的正确选项是 C。

28. C【解析】德国战舰受伤后指挥官决定逃向法国去维修，所以介词要用表示目的地方向的 to。

29. C【解析】at times 意为"有时，不时"，sometimes 意为"有时"，at that time 意为"在那时"，all the time 意为"始终"。法国在第二次世界大战期间曾被德国占领。战斗发生在 1941 年，当时法国还在德国统治下，所以 Bismarck 战舰才会前往法国维修。因此，这里的时间状语应为 at that time。

30. B【解析】find 意为"发现"，follow 意为"跟随，追击"，watch 意为"监视，注视"，see 意为"看见"。Bismarck 战舰是要从战斗中逃离，不存在英军发现、监视或是看见它

---

① 1 海里 = 1 852 米。

的说法。文章要表达的意思是"英军追击它"。

31. D【解析】although 意为"虽然，尽管"，but 意为"但是"，therefore 意为"因此"，however 意为"但是，然而"。英军追击 Bismarck 战舰时，Bismarck 战舰因其航速和大雾而得以逃离。这里需要一个转折连词，可以排除选项 C。but 一般不用逗号与句子隔开，所以可以排除选项 B。although 一般接转折的前提部分，因此 although 用在这里不合适。however 可以用逗号与句子隔开而单独使用，因此本题的最佳选项是 D。

32. D【解析】white 意为"白色的"，big 意为"大的"，large 意为"大的"，heavy 意为"重的，阴沉的，巨大的"。与文中"大雾"对应的是 heavy fog。

33. B【解析】control 意为"控制"，lose control of 意为"失去对……的控制"。sight 意为"视力，视觉"。lose contact 意为"失去联系"。由于 Bismarck 战舰在大雾中逃脱，因此英国人是"看不见"它了。因此，正确选项是 lose sight of。

34. D【解析】couldn't 意为"不能"，managed to 意为"成功做成了某事"，was unable to 意为"没能做某事"，tried to 意为"尽力做某事"。从后面的 with no success 来看，英军并没有发现 Bismarck 战舰，所以 B 项不正确。由于本句两个分句间存在转折关系，所以选项 A 和 C 也不正确。因此，本题的最佳选项是 D。

35. A【解析】slow down 意为"慢下来"。本题的意思是"为了让 Bismarck 战舰慢下来，以使其他战舰能追上它，英军对它进行了空中打击。"

第三部分　阅读理解

A

36. C【解析】推断题。根据第五段中的"The United states did just that in the 1970s."可知，答案选 C。

37. A【解析】推断题。根据文章内容可知，由于此书的出现，人们改变了对 DDT 的看法，接着停止了对 DDT 的使用。因此可以断定，此书是谈论 DDT 对人们的危害。

38. D【解析】判断题。根据文章倒数第二段第一句"But many critics of DDT worry it will not be used with great care."及全段内容可知，有些科学家仍然反对使用 DDT，由此可见并不是所有的科学家都同意，答案选 D。

39. A【解析】理解题。根据"it"所在句前面的内容可知，这里的"it"指的是对 DDT 的使用，答案选 A。

40. A【解析】推断题。根据本文内容，人们对 DDT 从禁用到重新启用，说明人们对事物的认识是不断发展变化的。答案选 A。

B

41. A【解析】词义猜测题。男女大脑的思维在某些方面的差异是天生固有的。

42. C【解析】推理判断题。根据文章第五段可推断出选项中这类物体是以白色为限定范畴的，答案选 C。

43. B【解析】推理判断题。男性在推理和空间思维方面占优势，女性在提取大脑中储存的记忆信息方面占优势。答案选 B。

44. A【解析】细节理解题。根据文章第四段可知，文章只是说调查涉及老年人，但并非都是老年人，故排除 B。选项 D 不是造成调查结果不准确的原因。

45. B 【解析】主旨理解题。根据文章第一段可知。

C

46. C 【解析】推理判断题。由第一段第四句 "The thing I like best about them is that your money is going to a good cause..." （"我"最喜欢慈善商店的一点是你的钱用于有用的事业），可推断出 C 项为正确答案。"goodwill" 含义为 "好意"。

47. D 【解析】事实细节题。由第二段第二、三两句 "The famous charity's appeal to aid postwar Greece had been so successful..." 可知第一个慈善商店的建立是为了筹钱援助战后的希腊。而从文章的第一段可知作者是英国人。因此，D 项正确。文章中未提 C 项中的 "patients"。

48. A 【解析】事实细节题。由第四段第一句 "The shops have very low running costs..." 可知 A 项正确。"running" 相当于 "operating"，含义为 "运营"，由第三段第一句中 "volunteer（志愿者）" 可知 B 项不正确。由第三段第二句可知慈善商店中 90% 以上的商品为公众捐赠，但并不能推出是 "二手货"，故 C 项不正确。文章中未提 D 项。

49. C 【解析】主旨大意题。本文的最后一句为主题句。由 "a good moral sense（好的道德感）" 和 "You provide funds to a good cause...（你为一项有意义的事业提供资金……）" 可知 C 项为最佳题目。"Charity Shop：Where You Buy to Donate（慈善商店——一个买东西就相当于捐款的地方）"

D

50. B 【解析】事实判断题。根据第一段第二句可知。

51. A 【解析】判断推理题。由第四段第一句 "To talk, you and I," 可知，此处是对上文 "He was quite happy and said, 'Great opportunity.'" 的解释。

52. B 【解析】细节推理题。文章结尾 grandpa 所说的话表明了态度。

E

53. C 【解析】文章最后点明了作者同意的观点，北京的经济会照样发展，不会受到很大的冲击。

54. C 【解析】文章第二段最后说到他认为中国是一个经济大国，奥运会的负面影响就像蚂蚁咬到龙身上，不会有什么感觉。

55. D 【解析】文章主要讲了专家对奥运会后北京及全国经济发展的看法。

第四部分 写　　作

第一节　短文改错

56. changed→changing
57. which→in which（where）
58. too→either
59. limit→limited
60. grown→grew
61. 去掉 an

62. √

63. name→names

64. new→of new

65. introduced→were introduced

第二节　书面表达

Dear editor,

  Nowadays video games are becoming more and more popular among the school students. Some students are so interested in the games that they spend all day playing. Sometimes they forget to do their homework and some even play truant. Each time they have to pay much money. As a result, they often ask their parents for more money, some borrow money from other students, and some even steal money from their classmates, which have very bad effects.

  Video game playing needs time, money and energy. It's not good for the students' study and health. I do hope measures will be taken by the government to prevent students from playing video games.

Yours ever,

Li Ming

Unit 2

Books

Part One Listening Practice

Section A

1. C 2. A 3. D 4. C 5. B

Section B

6. A 7. B 8. C 9. D 10. C

Section C

11) share 12) find out 13) are looking for
14) useful 15) be sure

Section D

1) books 2) mine 3) Be my guest
4) a fan 5) the reviews

Part Two Detailed Reading

译 文

圣杯之谜

《达·芬奇密码》是一部非常优秀的悬疑小说。因为小说的情节像电脑游戏一样紧张刺激，所以作者丹·布朗一定打过或者至少熟悉电脑游戏。小说中的情节险象环生，主角必须破解一系列谜题才可脱险，而他们解决了一个难题后马上又陷入另一个难题之中。

书中的两位主角是罗伯·兰登和索菲·纳芙。罗伯是一位哈佛大学的教授，宗教符号学方面的专家；而索菲是一位密码学家，供职于巴黎警局。作者这样安排角色，绝不是偶然的，二人合作可以成功地破解谜题，至少是书中提及的谜题。

开篇引人入胜。卢浮宫的馆长雅克·索尼埃被一名叫赛拉斯的修士枪击，腹部受伤后慢慢失血而死。雅克·索尼埃恰好是索菲·纳芙的祖父，当然这是作者早已设置好的。

雅克在临终之前写下了最初的谜题。他的遗体被发现时平躺在地板上，双手与双脚伸展开，雅克用自己的血写下了留给孙女索菲的加密信息。由于此案的警长贝祖·法希认为罗伯·兰登是凶手，所以罗伯·兰登被牵涉到案件之中。索菲知道罗伯是无辜的，便帮助他逃出卢浮宫，于是上演了一幕警察追击和破解谜题的剧情。

小说情节转换惊险刺激，谜题环环相扣，解决谜题的方法精妙无比，有些甚至极富创意。小说围绕着学者对耶稣（基督教的耶稣）的一种看法为中心展开剧情，他们认为耶稣有一段爱情故事甚至与抹大拉的玛丽亚结了婚，而当耶稣被钉死在十字架上之时，抹大拉的玛丽亚已经怀有身孕，这一点早已为教会所知却被教会精心掩盖起来。主角们为了圣杯的所在地秘密而被追杀，有一个神秘组织的成员知晓这一秘密，组织的成员就包括列奥纳多·达·芬奇。在小说情节的设置下，圣杯不是耶稣最后晚餐时所用的酒杯，而是比喻抹大拉的玛丽亚。她怀有耶稣的后代"圣杯"：她才是真正的圣杯。

读者要是对蒙娜·丽莎的神秘微笑或者对达·芬奇《最后的晚餐》人物里有一个女人这一惊人"事实"感兴趣的话，一定要读读《达·芬奇密码》。

Comprehension of the Text

1. B   2. C   3. C   4. B   5. D

Unit 2

 Part Three Exercises

Task 1

1. e   2. j   3. h   4. a   5. g
6. c   7. d   8. i   9. f   10. b

Task 2

1. puzzled   2. spread   3. expert   4. presented   5. fascinated
6. innocent   7. agent   8. intellectual 9. plot   10. case

Task 3

1. I'm well aware that very few jobs are available.
2. Her reply puzzled me.
3. I feel like going outdoors and spreading myself.
4. The murder case will be heard in the court next week.
5. He declared that he was innocent.

Task 4

A) Write a greeting card to your mother on Mother's Day.

> To my dearest Mom
>
> Happy Mother's Day
>
> You Were, Are and Will Always Be
> My Source of Power
>
> from your daughter

B) Write a greeting card to your friend Liu Qiang to congratulate on his success in the job interview.

To dear Liu Qiang

Congratulations on Your Success
In the Job Interview

from Li Hua

Part Four   Supplementary Reading

译　文

怎样提高阅读效率？

提高阅读效率有助于读者在短时间内明白作者所要传达的信息，也使读者心中目标明确，只读相关的材料即可。阅读时，要谨记良好的阅读方法总是伴随着做笔记的良好习惯。

提高阅读效率，首先要选择适合的方法来阅读各种不同的书籍。阅读的目的一般包括下列几项：从文章中获取信息；学习某一特定的题目或理论；准备考试。

在上述情况中，文章的性质就已经决定了阅读的方法。例如，读课本的方法就与读期刊、论文的方法不同。下面讨论三种书籍的阅读方法。

学术性的文章一般在形式和风格上都相对正式，一般是教科书或者课文。读一遍这类文章，要增加所获取的信息量，需要采用高效的学术文章阅读方法。可通过阅读前言找寻主题或总论，可从目录页综览全文或全书，还可以浏览主题句，这类句子概述了整段的观点，通常出现在段落的开头。

阅读有关细则，比如读如何护理病人的文章时，可使用多种方法。可通过文章的章、节和小节三级标题来把握整体的结构，也可快速阅读小节部分获取知识。要抓住段落的主旨句，因为主旨句概括了段落的观点、看法或者总体的想法。

期刊论文的结构一般很严谨，由期刊的种类与所报道的研究内容所决定，这便使得读者有时从中获取信息要比其他没那么严谨的文章要容易些。研究报告大部分都遵循特定的格式，包括摘要、引言、方法、结果、讨论和结论。

Comprehension of the Text

1. The purposes in reading might include: gathering information for an essay; learning about a particular topic or understanding a particular theory; preparing for an exam.
2. There are three types of books and they are academic books, textbooks and journals.

3. a. We can read the introduction to search for the thesis point or main argument.
   b. We can verify the overview provided by the contents page.
   c. Or we can scan by topic sentences, i. e. which is usually the first sentence of the paragraph.

自我测试题

第一部分　单项填空

从 [A]、[B]、[C]、[D] 四个选项中，选出可以填入空白处的最佳选项，并在答题卡上将该项涂黑。

> **Example:**
> It is generally considered unwise to give a child _____ he or she wants.
> [A] however　　　[B] whatever　　　[C] whichever　　　[D] whenever
> **Answer:** [A] [■] [C] [D]

1. The old movie reminded them _____ the wonderful time they had spent together.
   [A] to　　　　　　[B] for　　　　　　[C] in　　　　　　[D] of

2. When the city was _____, everyone knew that total defeat was certain.
   [A] cut off　　　[B] cut down　　　[C] cut across　　　[D] cut out

3. The Atlantic Ocean is over 6,000km _____ where Christopher Columbus crossed it.
   [A] deep　　　　[B] wide　　　　[C] long　　　　[D] across

4. —I heard that someone had got a full mark.
   —It _____ Li Ming. He worked really hard before the test.
   [A] has to be　　[B] will be　　[C] must be　　[D] could be

5. —Do you like the _____?
   —Sure, I do. Actually, I have four, too.
   [A] cups of coffee　[B] coffee's cups　[C] cups for coffee　[D] coffee cups

6. The picture brought the days back to me _____ I was studying at Peking University.
   [A] until　　　　[B] that　　　　[C] when　　　　[D] where

7. I prefer a university in Beijing to _____ in Shanghai, because Beijing is the cultural center of China.
   [A] one　　　　　[B] that　　　　[C] it　　　　　[D] this

8. Li Ming is said _____ in Beijing, but I don't know which hotel he stays in.
   [A] to be on a business trip
   [B] to have been on a business trip
   [C] to on a business trip
   [D] to being on a business

9. Please pay a visit to us, _____ you come to this city.

[A] whichever　　[B] however　　[C] whatever　　[D] whenever

10. After a serious earthquake, a lot of buildings _____.

　　[A] are damaged　[B] had damaged　[C] damaged　[D] were damaged

11. —I will have several final exams next week.

　　—_____!

　　[A] Congratulations　[B] Cheers　[C] Best wishes　[D] Good luck

12. —I think Li Ming's performance was excellent.

　　—_____.

　　[A] So it was　[B] So was it　[C] So was he　[D] So he was

13. I'd like to arrive 20 minutes early _____ I can have time for a cup of tea.

　　[A] as soon as　[B] as a result　[C] in case　[D] so that

14. To our delight, she quickly _____ herself to the situation.

　　[A] adopted　[B] adapted　[C] attached　[D] appealed

15. I couldn't do my homework with all that noise _____.

　　[A] going on　[B] goes on　[C] went on　[D] to go on

第二部分　完形填空

阅读下面短文，从短文后所给的四个选项（[A]、[B]、[C]、[D]）中选出能填入相应空白处的最佳选项，并在答题卡上将该项涂黑。

It was a cold winter's afternoon. Robert stopped for a moment when he crossed the bridge and looked down at the river below. There were hardly any __16__ on the river. __17__ the bridge, however, almost directly below, __18__ was a small canoe (独木舟), with a boy in it. He was __19__ wearing many clothes, Robert __20__. He shivered (打了个寒战) and walked on.

　__21__ he heard a cry. "Help! Help!" The cry __22__ from the river. Robert looked down. The boy was __23__ the water and his canoe was __24__ away. "Help! Help!" he called again.

　Robert was a good __25__. Taking off his clothes, he __26__ into the river. The __27__ water made him tremble all over, __28__ in a few seconds he reached the __29__. "Don't be afraid!" he said and started to swim towards the river bank, __30__ the boy with him. But at that __31__ he noticed a large motor boat under the bridge. There were several people on the boat, all __32__ in his direction. Robert __33__ to swim towards the boat.

　"Give me a hand," he shouted __34__ he got near the boat. He __35__ up into a row of faces. "It's funny," he thought. "They look so angry." Silently they helped the boy into the boat and wrapped him in a blanket. But they did not move to help Robert.

　"Aren't you going to pull me out, too?" Robert asked.

　"You!" said one of the men. Robert noticed that he was standing next to a large camera, "You! Why, we were making a film and you spoiled (破坏) a whole afternoon's work! You can stay in the water!"

16. [A] fish   [B] boats   [C] waves   [D] sounds
17. [A] From   [B] Towards   [C] Near   [D] Beyond
18. [A] there   [B] it   [C] where   [D] that
19. [A] then   [B] also   [C] only   [D] not
20. [A] noticed   [B] saw   [C] guessed   [D] said
21. [A] Till then [B] Just then [C] Far away   [D] From there
22. [A] happened [B] went   [C] arrived   [D] came
23. [A] on   [B] within   [C] in   [D] under
24. [A] running   [B] floating   [C] flowing   [D] pulling
25. [A] swimmer   [B] guard   [C] soldier   [D] sportsman
26. [A] threw   [B] looked   [C] dived   [D] turned
27. [A] deep   [B] cool   [C] dirty   [D] cold
28. [A] but   [B] so   [C] and   [D] or
29. [A] canoe   [B] bank   [C] boy   [D] bridge
30. [A] pushing   [B] dragging   [C] holding   [D] catching
31. [A] place   [B] period   [C] second   [D] moment
32. [A] seeing   [B] smiling   [C] looking   [D] shouting
33. [A] decided   [B] went   [C] agreed   [D] promised
34. [A] while   [B] till   [C] for   [D] as
35. [A] turned   [B] looked   [C] hurried   [D] stood

第三部分 阅读理解

阅读下列短文，从每题所给的四个选项（[A]、[B]、[C]、[D]）中选出最佳选项，并在答题卡上将该项涂黑。

A

It seems that politicians around the world are thinking about the health of their countries. While in China, Chen Zhu has announced his plans for a universal health service and reform across health services. Gordon Brown, the UK Prime Minister, has also announced he is planning to make some changes in our health service.

The crux of Mr. Brown's proposals are related to giving the NHS (National Health Service) a greater focus on prevention, rather than just curing patients.

He is planning to introduce increased screening for common diseases such as heart disease, strokes, and cancer, for example, breast cancer. In Britain there are 200,000 deaths a year from heart attacks and strokes, many of which might have been avoided if the condition had been known about.

Initially, the diagnostic (诊断的) tests will be available for those who are vulnerable, or most likely to have the disease, but later on the Prime Minister claims that they will be more widely available. One example is a plan to offer all men over 65 an ultrasound test to check for problems with the main artery (动脉), a condition which kills 3,000 men a year.

The opposition has criticized Mr. Brown's proposals, saying that they are just a trick, and claiming that there is no proper timetable for the changes. They also say that Mr. Brown is reducing the money available for the treatment of certain conditions while putting more money towards testing for them.

The NHS was founded in 1948, and is paid for by taxation. The idea is that the rich pay more towards the health service than the poor. However in recent years there has been a great increase in the use of private healthcare, because it's much quicker. NHS waiting lists for operations can be very long, so many people who can afford it choose to pay for medical care themselves.

36. The underlined word "vulnerable" in the fourth paragraph probably means _____.
    [A] sick   [B] weak   [C] wounded   [D] old
37. All the following statements are true EXCEPT that _____.
    [A] all people should pay for their healthcare at the NHS
    [B] some people are against the reform of the healthcare
    [C] the writer is likely to come from Britain
    [D] more money will be spent on testing people than before
38. Which of the following is the reason for the increasing private healthcare?
    [A] People are paying more attention to their own health.
    [B] People are well-off enough to pay their healthcare.
    [C] The NHS was not available for most of the people.
    [D] It's not so convenient for people to go to the NHS for their healthcare.
39. According to the passage, the purpose of the health reform plan in the UK is to _____
    [A] encourage more private healthcare
    [B] focus on the prevention rather than on curing the patient
    [C] deal with the main artery problems
    [D] fight against the opposition in the UK
40. The author of this passage intends to tell us _____.
    [A] the NHS should be reformed right away
    [B] more and more people are dying from diseases
    [C] the plan to reform the NHS in the UK
    [D] the criticism of Mr. Brown's proposals

B

When it comes to friends, I desire those who will share my happiness, who possess wings of their own and who will fly with me. I seek friends whose qualities illuminate (照亮) me and train me up for love. It is for these people that I reserve the glowing hours, too good not to share.

When I was in the eighth grade, I had a friend. We were shy and "too serious" about our studies when it was becoming fashionable with our classmates to learn acceptable social behaviors. We said little at school, but she would come to my house and we would sit down with pencils and paper, and one of us would say: "Let's start with a train whistle today." We would sit quietly together and write separate poems or stories that grew out of a train whistle. Then we would read them aloud. At the end of that school year, we, too, were changing into social creatures and the stories and poems stopped.

When I lived for a time in London, I had a friend. He was in despair and I was in despair. But our friendship was based on the idea in each of us that we would be sorry later if we did not explore this great city because we had felt bad at the time. We met every Sunday for five weeks and found many excellent things. We walked until our despairs disappeared and then we parted. We gave London to each other.

For almost four years I have had remarkable friend whose imagination illuminates mine. We write long letters in which we often discover our strangest selves. Each of us appears, sometimes in a funny way, in the other's dreams. She and I agree that, at certain times, we seem to be parts of the same mind. In my most interesting moments, I often think: "Yes, I must tell…" We have never met.

It is such comforting companions I wish to keep. One bright hour with their kind is worth more to me than the lifetime services of a psychologist, who will only fill up the healing (愈合的) silence necessary to those darkest moments in which I would rather be my own best friend.

41. In the eighth grade, what the author did before developing proper social behavior was to _____.

   [A] become serious about her study
   [B] go to her friend's house regularly
   [C] learn from her classmates at school
   [D] share poems and stories with her friend

42. In Paragraph 3, "We gave London to each other" probably means _____
   [A] our exploration of London was a memorable gift to both of us
   [B] we were unwilling to tear ourselves away from London
   [C] our unpleasant feeling about London disappeared
   [D] we parted with each other in London

43. According to Paragraph 4, the author and her friend _____
   [A] call each other regularly   [B] have similar personalities
   [C] enjoy writing to each other   [D] dream of meeting each other

44. In the darkest moments, the author would prefer to _____.
   [A] seek professional help   [B] be left alone
   [C] stay with her best friend   [D] break the silence

45. What is the best title for the passage?
   [A] Unforgettable Experiences   [B] Remarkable Imagination

[C] Lifelong Friendship   [D] Noble Companions

C

O. Henry was an American short-story writer, a master of surprising endings, who wrote about the life of ordinary people in New York city. A twist of plot, which turns on an ironic or coincidental circumstance, is typical of O. Henry's stories.

William Sydney Porter (O. Henry) was born in North Carolina. His father was a physician. When William was three, his mother died, and he was raised by his grandmother and aunt. At the age of fifteen he left school, and then worked in a drug store. He moved to Houston, where he had a number of jobs, including that of bank clerk. After moving to Austin, Texas, in 1882, he married.

In 1884 he started a humorous weekly The Rolling Stone. When the weekly failed, he joined the *Houston Post* as a reporter and columnist. In 1897 he was convicted of embezzling money, although there has been much debate over his actual guilt.

While in prison O. Henry started to write short stories to earn money to support his daughter Margaret. His first work, Whistling Dick's Christmas Stocking (1899), appeared in Mcclure's Magazine. After doing three years of the five years sentence, Porter emerged from the prison in 1901 and changed his name to O. Henry.

O. Henry moved to New York city in 1902 and from December 1903 to January 1906 he wrote a story a week for the New York world, also publishing in other magazines. Henry's first collection, *Cabbages and Kings* appeared in 1904. The second, *The Four Million*, was published two years later and included his well-known stories *The Gift of the Magi* and *The Furnished Room*. O. Henry published 10 collections and over 600 short stories during his lifetime.

O. Henry's last years were shadowed by ill health and financial problems. He married Sara Lindsay Coleman in 1907, but the marriage was not happy, and they separated one year later. O. Henry died on June 5, 1910, in New York.

46. The following statements are the characteristics of O. Henry's stories EXCEPT _____.
    [A] the stories often end with surprising endings
    [B] there are a lot of coincidences in his stories
    [C] the stories are mainly about common people
    [D] his own experiences are main subjects in his stories

47. We can infer from the text that _____.
    [A] O. Henry's mother's death resulted in his leaving school
    [B] O. Henry earned much money by starting the weekly
    [C] some people believed O. Henry was put in prison for no good reason
    [D] his daughter asked O. Henry to write short stories

48. One of O. Henry's most famous story *The Gift of the Magi* came out in _____.
    [A] 1902   [B] 1904   [C] 1906   [D] 1907

49. What do you think of O. Henry's life?

[A] Rough.   [B] Smooth.   [C] Rich.   [D] Happy.

D

The snow has paralyzed transport in China during the country's most important vacation period, the celebration of the Chinese New Year. Not only have transport delays hindered personal trips, but they have also slowed the delivery of fresh produce to markets. Consequently, in Zhengzhou, the capital city of the Henan province, tomato prices have doubled, and the cost of 47 other vegetables has increased by 36%, as reported by local media at the end of January.

According to an inside PR source, "Wholesalers in Beijing were quoted as saying that only about 20% of the usual fresh vegetable supplies were reaching the city." As an Asian country with a diet based on fresh produce, the shortage of vegetables and the rise in prices is not only affecting fresh food producers, but also the final consumers.

In terms of production, this is the worst snow disaster to hit China in the last 50 years, affecting a total of 9.4 million hectares of farmland in the country, according to a report published on 4 February 2008 by Feng Tao of Xinhua News, at the Chinese government website. Most of the crops devastated (毁坏) by the frost are located in the middle and lower reaches of the Yangtze River, the traditional natural border between North and South China.

Chen Xiwen, Director of the Office of the Central Leading Group on Rural Work, pointed out at the end of last week that "the blizzard disaster in the south has had a severe impact on winter crops, and the impact on fresh vegetables could be catastrophic in certain areas," as stated in the Xinhua News report.

The Chinese government has been quick to take extreme measures. The Chinese Ministry of Agriculture (MOA) has sent 13 teams of experts to 8 of the areas most seriously affected by the harsh weather. The aim of this initiative is to provide farmers with technical assistance to minimize their losses.

50. From this passage, we can know that the snow happened _____.
    [A] during the Spring Festival   [B] in the coldest days of the winter
    [C] in the North of China   [D] It's not mentioned here

51. What's the meaning of the underlined word "blizzard" in paragraph four?
    [A] Worst.   [B] Snowstorm.   [C] Cold weather.   [D] Biggest.

52. This passage mainly tells us _____.
    [A] the snow in the south of China caused many problems
    [B] the effect of the snow in the south of China on the fresh food
    [C] the snow in the south of China slowed the delivery of fresh produce to markets
    [D] the Chinese government has taken extreme measures to help the suffered farmers

E

We experience different forms of the Sun's energy every day. We can see its light and feel its warmth. The Sun is the major source of energy for our planet. It causes the evaporation (蒸发)

of water from the oceans and lakes. Sunlight also provides the energy used by green plants to make their own food. These green plants then provide food for all organisms on the Earth.

Much of the energy that comes from the Sun never reaches the Earth's surface. It is either reflected or absorbed by the gases in the upper atmosphere. Of the energy that reaches the lower atmosphere, 30% is reflected by clouds or the Earth's surface. The remaining 70% warms the surface of the planet, causes water to evaporate, and provides energy for the water cycle and weather. Only a tiny part, approximately 0.023%, is actually used by green plants to produce food.

Many gases found in the atmosphere actually reflect heat energy escaping from the Earth's surface back to the Earth. These gases act like the glass of a greenhouse in that they allow energy from the Sun to enter but prevent energy from leaving. They are therefore called greenhouse gases.

When sunlight strikes an object, some of the energy is absorbed and some is reflected. The amount reflected depends on the surface. For example, you've probably noticed how bright snow is when sunlight falls on it. Snow reflects most of the energy from the Sun, so it contributes to the low temperatures of winter. Dark-colored surfaces, such as dark soil or forest, absorb more energy and help warm the surrounding air.

53. According to the passage, the root cause for weather changes on the Earth is _____.

　　[A] the atmosphere surrounding the Earth　　[B] water from oceans and lakes
　　[C] energy from the Sun　　[D] greenhouse gases in the sky

54. Only a small part of the Sun's energy reaches the Earth's surface because most of it is _____.

　　[A] absorbed by the clouds in the lower atmosphere
　　[B] reflected by the gases in the upper atmosphere
　　[C] lost in the upper and lower atmosphere
　　[D] used to evaporate water from the oceans and lakes

55. We learn from the passage that _____.

　　[A] all living things on the Earth depend on the Sun for their food
　　[B] a forest looks dark in winter because it absorbs solar energy
　　[C] only 0.023% of the energy from the Sun is made use of on the Earth
　　[D] greenhouse gases allow heat energy to escape from the Earth's surface

第四部分　写　　作

第一节　短文改错

此题要求改正所给短文中的错误。对标有题号的每一行做出判断：如无错误，在该行右边横线上画一个勾（√）；如有错误（每行只有一个错误），则按下列情况改正：

此行多一个词：把多余的词用斜线（＼）划掉，在该行右边横线上写出该词，并也用斜线划掉。

此行缺一个词：在缺词处加一个漏字符号（∧），在该行右边横线上写出该加的词。
此行错一个词：在错的词下画一横线，在该行右边横线上写出改正后的词。
注意：原行没有错的不要改。

Every morning John goes to work by trains. He　　　　　　56._____
always buys a newspaper, it helps to make the time　　　　57._____
pass more quickly. One Thursday morning, he turned on the sports　58._____
page. He wanted to see the report about an important　　　59._____
football match the night before. The report was such　　　60._____
interesting that he forgot to get off at his station. He didn't know it
when he saw the sea. He got off at the　　　　　　　　　　61._____
next station, and had to wait long time for a train to　　　62._____
go back. Of course, he arrived very late at the office.　　　63._____
His boss were very angry when Tom told him why he was late.　64._____
"Work is very more important than football!" he shouted.　65._____

第二节　书面表达

假定你是李明，你从网上得知一位美国中学生 Tom 很想交中国朋友。恰好你也有同样的愿望，很想与其通信，成为笔友。请你根据以下提示写封回信。

要点：
1. 简单的自我介绍（学校、学校课程、课外安排及老师情况等）；
2. 询问对方的情况及学校生活；
3. 表达愿望，希望能够成为好朋友。

注意：词数 100 个左右。

参考答案及解析

第一部分　单项填空

1. D【解析】remind sb. of sth. 是一个固定搭配，意思是"使某人想起某物或某事"，介词一定用 of，故选 D。

2. A【解析】cut off 意为"切断"，cut down 意为"砍倒"，cut across 意为"抄近路"，cut out 意为"切掉"。本题的意思是"城市与外界的联系被切断了，所有人都知道失败在所难免"，故选 A。

3. B【解析】deep 表示深度，wide 表示宽度和广度，long 表示长度，across 意为"横过"。本题说的是大西洋的宽度，故选 B。

4. C【解析】第一个说话人听说有人得了满分，而第二个说话人提供了"李明考试前学习非常刻苦"这一信息，所以第二个说话人的意思"得满分的一定是李明"，"must do"在这里表示肯定推测，故选 C。

5. D【解析】本题要确定的是第一个说话人喜欢的是咖啡还是咖啡杯。第二个人回答中有 I have four，可见两个人谈论的是咖啡杯，正确的答案在 B 和 D 之间。名词可以直接用作定语，而且我们也常用 coffee cup 来表示"咖啡杯"，故选 D。

6. C【解析】本题考查定语从句的用法。_____ I was studying at Peking University 用来修饰先行词 the days，相当于 during which，因此我们应该用表示时间的关系副词 when。

7. A【解析】代词对应的名词是 university，并且是不确定的指代，因此填入空白处的应是 one。

8. A【解析】选项 C 缺少一个动词，选项 D 没有用动词原形，因此这两项可以排除。从题干第二个分句来看，李明仍在北京。B 项中不定式 to have been on a business trip 用的是过去时，A 项中 to be on a business trip 是一般现在时，故选 A。

9. D【解析】本题解题的关键在于理解题意，题中句子的意思是"不论你什么时候到本市，请一定拜访我们"。因此，应填 whenever。

10. D【解析】事情发生在过去，应该用一般过去时；建筑是被毁坏，因此必须用被动语态。综合上述两个因素，应填 were damaged，故选 D。

11. D【解析】第一个说话人说下周有几门考试，第二个说话人得体的反应是祝他好运，因此应用 Good luck。

12. A【解析】第一个说话人认为"李明的表演非常出色"，谈论的是"李明的表演"，而不是"李明"，所以我们应该用 it 作代词。第二个说话人是在附和第一个说话人的看法，因此我们要用"so+主语+助动词"的句型，故选 A。

13. D【解析】as soon as 意为"一……就……"。as a result 意为"结果"，通常要用逗号与句子隔开，单独使用。in case 意为"万一"。so that 意为"以便"，表示目的，它引导的从句中一般要用 can、could 等情态动词。本句的意思是"我想提前 20 分钟到达，以便喝杯茶"，故选 D。

14. B【解析】adopt 意为"采用，收养"，adapt 意为"使适应，改编"，attach 意为"系上，贴上，隶属于"，appeal 意为"请示，呼吁"。本句的意思是"令我们高兴的是，他很快就适应了形势"，故选 B。

15. A【解析】本题考查"with+动词过去分词/v. +-ing 形式"的结构。这里 noise 是 go 的动作发出者，所以这里我们要用表示主动意义的"v. +-ing"的形式，故选 A。

第二部分　完形填空

16. B【解析】后面一句话中有 however 一词，因此与本句存在转折关系。那一句话的意思是"桥下有一只独木舟"。与此相对应，本句应该是说河上没有任何船只。因此，本题的正确答案是 B。

17. C【解析】从后面 Robert 跳水救人的情节来看，独木舟离桥应该不远。因此，本题的正确选项是 C。

18. A【解析】本题考查 there be 句型的用法。如果用 it，那么这个 it 就存在指代不明的问题；如果用 that，也存在与 it 同样的问题；如果用 where，那么句子就缺少一个主语。因此，本题的正确答案是 A。

19. D【解析】我们从下文知道，这个孩子是在演落水的戏，所以身上应该没有穿多少衣服，这样才有利于随时开拍。因此，本题的正确答案是 D。

20. A【解析】这一幕是 Robert 亲眼所见的，所以选项 C 和 D 可以排除。notice 意为"注意到"，see 意为"看见"。从意思上看，前者更切合文意。

21. B【解析】在本句话的后面有一句 Robert looked down，既然此时他还能从桥上往下看，那么他还没有走出多远，就听到了"救命"声。因此，本题的正确答案是 B。

22. D【解析】本题要表达的意思是"喊声来自于河上"。happen 意为"发生"，go 意为"去，离开"，arrive 意为"到达"。这三个词都不能与 from 连用。come 意为"来"，可以与介词 from 搭配。

23. C【解析】从下文来看，小孩子落水了，而在水里是 in the water。因此，本题的正确答案为 C。

24. B【解析】小孩落水后，独木舟上没有人，所以会自行漂走。run 意为"跑"，float 意为"漂"，flow 意为"流"，pull 意为"拉"。因此，本题的正确答案是 B。

25. A【解析】swimmer 意为"游泳者"，guard 意为"保卫"，soldier 意为"战士"，sportsman 意为"运动员"。联系下文看，Robert 下水救人，所以他应该是一名"游泳健将"，因此，本题的正确答案是 A。

26. C【解析】Robert 脱了衣服，然后就要跳到河中救人。throw 意为"扔，抛"，look 意为"看"，dive 意为"跳水，下潜"，turn 意为"转动，转变方向"。因此，正确选项为 C。

27. D【解析】解决本题的关键是 tremble 一词，它的意思是"颤抖"，由此判断水应该是非常冷的。因此，本题的正确答案是 D。

28. A【解析】由于这个句子中两个分句的主谓结构是完整的，所以属于并列句，我们需要找一个并列连词。鉴于两个分句间存在一种转折关系，but 更为合适。因此，本题的正确答案是 A。

29. C【解析】紧接着本句话的是 Robert 对落水男孩说的话，所以本句中他应该游到了孩子的身边。因此，本题的正确答案是 C。

30. B【解析】push 意为"推"，drag 意为"拖，拽"，hold 意为"拿着，持有"，catch 意为"抓住，捕获"。在水中救人时，我们一般是要拖着落水人往前游，应该用 drag。

31. D【解析】at that moment 是一个固定搭配，意为"就在那个时候"。

32. C【解析】本句的意思是"船上的所有人都朝他们这个方向看着"。see 是及物动词，不能用在这里。smile 和 shout 两个词的意思不符。因此，本题的正确答案是 C。

33. A【解析】decide 意为"决定"，go 意为"离开，走开"，agree 意为"达成协议，同意"，promise 意为"承诺，保证"。从意思上来看，decide 最为确切。因此，本题的正确选项是 A。

34. D【解析】while 意为"当……时候，虽然"，till 意为"直到，在……之前"，for 意为"因为"，as 意为"当……时候"。while 表示时间段，而 as 表示一种伴随状态，暗含"一边……一边……"的意思。因此，as 填入文中更为合适。

35. B【解析】turn 意为"出现，突然发生"，look up 意为"向上看，仰望，查寻"，hurry up 意为"赶快"，stand up 意为"站起来"。Robert 在水中要想看到船上人的脸就得向上看，所以要用 look up。

第三部分 阅读理解

A

36. B【解析】词义猜测题。根据其后一句"or most likely to have the disease"可知此处为"体弱者"。

37. A【解析】细节理解题。根据文章最后一段可知，能够负担得起费用的人们常常自己花钱去看病，这也就是说人们本来可以不用花钱的。故选项 A 不正确，为答案。选项 B 根据文章倒数第二段可知，反对党对这个建议进行了批判；选项 C 根据文章第一段最后一句可知；选项 D 根据文章倒数第二段最后一句可反推出来。

38. D【解析】细节理解题。根据文章最后一段可知，人们自己掏钱看病的原因是因为在 NHS 的等待时间太长，所以对人们来说不方便，答案选 D。

39. B【解析】细节理解题。根据文章第二段可知。

40. C【解析】主旨大意题。根据文章第一段最后一句可知。事实上，本文作者重点介绍了英国的医疗改革计划，文章大量篇幅都在说明英国的医疗状况。

B

41. D【解析】细节推断题。从第二段倒数第三行文字可以看出，他和同学在一起写诗和文章，然后诵读。在学期结束时，他们才形成适当的社交行为。与此同时，他们也停止了写诗和文章的活动了。

42. A【解析】推断题。从第三段第二句可以看出，他们持有同样的看法。如果他们不走遍 (explore) 整个伦敦城，他们就不会高兴。从本段的最后一句看出，他们不停地在这座城市里散步，直到他们的失望感消失，才各自离开。

43. C【解析】细节推断题。从第四段可以看出，他们经常相互写信，但从来没有见过面。

44. C【解析】细节推断题。从最后一段可以看出，在作者情绪最低落的时候，作者希望自己最好的朋友呆在身边。(...those darkest moments in which I would rather be my own best friend.)

45. D【解析】主旨题。整篇文章表达的是作者在不同时期的朋友伴随自己成长变化的过程。说明了朋友对自己的影响和崇高的友谊。

C

46. D【解析】仔细阅读第一段会发现，这段包含了 A、B、C 三个选项的内容。只有 D 项文章没有提及，所以它不是 O. Henry 的写作特点。

47. C【解析】根据第二段第三句 "When William was three, his mother died" 知道，母亲死时他才 3 岁，而辍学是 15 岁，两者没有必然联系；第三段的第二句 "the weekly failed"，说明他并没有赚到钱；第四段第一句 "While in prison O. Henry started to write short stories to earn money to support his daughter Margaret." 可知，O. Henry 是为了抚养女儿写作，不是女儿要求他写作，所以 A、B、D 都是错误选项。从第三段的最后一句 "although there has been much debate over his actual guilt." 可以推测，有人认为他有罪，也有人认为他没有罪。答案选 C。

48. C【解析】第五段的倒数第二句 "two years later and included his well-known stories *The Gift of the Magi*" 可以推算，这篇小说是在 1906 年出版的。

49. A【解析】(根据第二段可知) O. Henry 经历了孤独的童年，艰难的青年时期；(第三段中可知) 经过了艰辛的创业；(第四段中) 又遭牢狱之灾；(第五段中) 尽管后期作品很受欢迎，(第六段中) 但又忍受疾病之苦，婚姻不幸，可谓命运多舛。所以首先排除 C、D 两个选项；B 选项 smooth 意为"平坦的"与文章内容不符。只有 A 选项 rough 意为"崎岖不平的"，形容人生的坎坷。

D

50. A【解析】第一段开头提到时间是在庆祝新年期间。

Unit 2

51. B【解析】本文开头就提到大雪对人们产生的影响，可以看出发生的是雪灾。
52. B【解析】文章分析了大雪对农产品如蔬菜、水果的影响，C、D 只提了其中的一个方面，不全面。

E

53. C【解析】细节题。据第二段 "The remaining 70% warms the surface of the planet, causes water to evaporate, and provides energy for the water cycle and weather." 判断得出答案。
54. C【解析】细节题。据第二段 "Much of the energy... is either reflected or absorbed by the gases in the upper atmosphere. Of the energy that reaches the lower atmosphere, 30% is reflected by clouds or the Earth's surface." 可以得出答案。
55. A【解析】主旨题。通读全文不难看出文章是关于太阳能是如何被地球生物利用的。B、C、D 都有点以偏概全。

第四部分 写 作

第一节 短文改错

56. trains→ train
57. it→which
58. on→to
59. see→read
60. such→so
61. when→until
62. wait→wait a
63. √
64. were→was
65. very→much/去掉 very

第二节 书面表达

Dear Tom,

    I'm glad to read your letter on the Internet and I'd like to be your pen friend. I'm Li Ming, aged 17, and I'm a middle school student. At school we have Chinese, math, English, physics, chemistry and P. E. lessons. After school in the afternoon, we usually have sports and games. In the evening we do our lessons at school. We are busy but happy. In addition, our teachers are kind to us as well as strict with us. With their help, we have made great progress. We are proud of our school.

    Would you please tell me something about you and your school? I hope we will be good friends.

    Please write to me soon.

Yours truly,
Li Ming

Unit 3

Generation

 Part One Listening Practice

Section A

1. B	2. B	3. A	4. A	5. B
6. B	7. B	8. A	9. A	10. B
11. B	12. A	13. B	14. B	15. A
16. B	17. A	18. B	19. A	20. A

Section B

Task 1

1) 70 2) independent 3) get lonely
4) twice a week 5) too busy

Task 2

6) I've been meaning 7) How are things with you 8) So far so good
9) in the law office 10) how about your brother Dennis 11) Couldn't be better
12) action star

Part Two Detailed Reading

Y 一代的工作观

　　这些人青春无敌、聪明潇洒，在办公室里穿着人字拖走来走去，办公时开着 MP3，他们爱工作，但绝不让工作成为其生活的全部。

　　这就是 Y 一代，人数多达 7,000 万，第一波已经进入职场，这一代大多数还不到 30 岁，是前无古人的一代，公司老板们对此不知是否准备好了。

　　平衡工作与生活对于他们不只是说说而已。与上一代高度重视事业不同，今日 Y 一代更加注重工作要与家庭和私人生活相协调。工作对他们来说要有灵活性，等有了孩子他们可以做兼职或者暂时不工作。

　　家在旧金山的黛安娜·圣地亚哥，今年 24 岁，她在大学工作，还和父母住在一起，她说："现在我们对于成功有了更高的标准，'9·11 事件'之后，很多人都认识到生命很短暂，因此更加看重生活。"

　　改变多多益善。Y 一代不希望一直做一份工作，或者长期从事一种职业，他们早就洞悉了安然和安达信公司的财务丑闻，谈到所谓员工忠诚时他们实在是不以为然。

　　他们不愿意一直执行一项工作任务。这一代的人是多面手，他们上网时可以一边用手机打电话，一边用黑莓发邮件。

　　他们信奉自我的价值，珍视到足够令他们换公司时毫不胆怯。这些多少与 X 一代形成对比。X 一代，出生于 20 世纪 60 年代中期到 70 年代后期，善于独立思考，嗜好改变，重视家庭。

　　他们对有些着装要求与管理风格有抵触情绪。在工作场合，很多事情会产生矛盾，平添烦恼，甚至看起来不起眼的衣着方面也如此，因为 Y 一代习惯了休闲，如穿人字拖、七分裤，身上纹有刺青。

　　德州的阿尔文市的安吉·平，今年 23 岁，习惯了穿人字拖，但是他所在的公司禁止员工上班时间穿人字拖。他说："在这一季的职业装潮流中，设计师对男装的灵感大发，七分裤配上高跟鞋，穿起来和裤装一样华丽，可惜我所在的机构不让穿七分裤。"

　　在管理上，也有冲突出现。上一代的人在成长过程中做惯了年终总结，Y 一代却与他们不同，他们从小就习惯了与父母师长时常交流反馈，并得到认可。要是不能定期与老板沟通，他们便感到迷惑。所以现在是老板们解决这些矛盾的时候了。

　　Y 一代与其他年代的人不同。他们对工作持有不同的态度：他们对事情有不同的见解，但是会从中找到一个平衡点。

Comprehension of the Text

1. 1) Work-life balance isn't just a buzzword.
   2) Change, change, change.
   3) Conflicts over casual dress and management style.
2. Unlike older generations who tend to put a high priority on career, today's youngest workers are more interested in making their jobs fit their family and personal lives. They want jobs with flexibility. They want the ability to go part time or leave the workforce temporarily when children are in the picture.
3. They're doubtful when it comes to such ideas as employee loyalty.
4. They can manage to send e-mail on their BlackBerrys while talking on cellphones while surfing online.
5. Conflicts will appear in seemingly minor subjects such as appearance, and conflict can also emerge over management style.

Part Three Exercises

Task 1

| 1. g | 2. c | 3. e | 4. i | 5. d |
| 6. h | 7. a | 8. j | 9. f | 10. b |

Task 2

| 1. feedback | 2. accustomed | 3. addiction | 4. inspired | 5. conflict |
| 6. when it comes to | 7. emerged | 8. casual | 9. temporarily | 10. priority |

Task 3

1. This house doesn't <u>compare with</u> our previous one.
2. I'm not <u>used to</u> spicy food.
3. The sun <u>emerged</u> from behind the clouds.
4. <u>When it comes to</u> German, I know nothing.
5. She is a <u>career woman</u> rather than a housewife.

Task 4

Wet Floor	小心地滑
Entrance	入口
Booking Office	订票处
Two-way Street	双行线街道
Keep Off Lawn	请勿践踏草坪
No Spitting	不要随地吐痰
No Parking	禁止停车
Staff Only	员工专用
Hand With Care	小心轻放
Silence	肃静
Hands Off	请勿触摸
Road Construction Ahead	前方修路

Part Four Supplementary Reading

译文

EMO 青年遭袭击

2008年3月7日，大约800名年轻人冲入墨西哥城，到处找爱好EMO的青少年，试图要打他们。一些孩子被他们发现后就被暴打一番。整个场景非常可怕，电视新闻对此做了报道。这仅是针对EMO族群新的暴力浪潮的一瞥，墨西哥的EMO族群是近十年来逐渐发展形成起来的。EMO亚文化大概在这一称谓还未风行时就已经出现了，"80后"的哥特风和"90后"的摇滚风代表了这一亚文化的最新的动向。在学校的年鉴中能看到这些孩子，他们留着夸张的发型，沉湎于悲伤的音乐中。总之，这些孩子在这些年间经常被人殴打。

以前EMO流行于美国和欧洲有色人种的青少年中间，是青少年亚文化的一种。随着墨西哥的经济贸易与政治国际关系走向开放化，新的一代伴着网络与有线电视长大，现在已经席卷至格兰德河。朋克、哥特、乡村摇滚、霹雳舞、轮滑和重金属音乐的爱好者们都漫步在墨西哥的街头上，他们在广场游荡，在墙上喷洒油漆。但是EMO们的行为令很多人难以接受，激起了人们的强烈反对。本月前些天，据报道，一大群人在墨西哥城市中心殴打了EMO的青少年们。此外，EMO青少年们也抱怨说每日在街上都有小群的人威胁并袭击他们，这一情况正越来越严重。一群孩子坐在墨西哥城广场上，他们身着黑色紧身牛仔裤，化着很浓的妆，其中一位16岁的高中生说："现在我们出去时越来越危险，人们冲我们大喊，往我们身上吐唾沫，拿东西砸我们，恨我们的人太多了。"

袭击者，称作"反EMO"，包括一些从其他城市来的人，比如朋克、重金属音乐爱好者。但是许多"反EMO"是普通的劳动阶层的青年人，他们嘲笑EMO们多愁善感、装腔作势，指责他们抢了其他音乐流派的风头。20世纪80年代，EMO诞生于华盛顿，乐队在表演时借鉴了大量朋克和摇滚音乐的元素，专注于深入自己的情感（EMO由此得名），特别是抒发青年人独有的绝望感。

Comprehension of the Text

1. EMO youth culture is the culture of the generation who grow up with the Internet and Cable TV in the 1980s and 1990s and who are strongly influenced by rock music, punk and so on. They wear exaggerated haircut and immerse themselves in sad music.
2. They think EMO youth are too sentimental and accuse them of robbing from other music genres.
3. Other youth subcultures may include Net Radio Generation, Hip Hop, indie culture and so on.

自我测试题

第一部分　单项填空

从［A］、［B］、［C］、［D］四个选项中，选出可以填入空白处的最佳选项，并在答题卡上将该项涂黑。

Example：
　　It is generally considered unwise to give a child _____ he or she wants.
　　［A］however　　　［B］whatever　　　［C］whichever　　　［D］whenever
Answer：　［A］　［■］　［C］　［D］

1. When Mark opened the door, he saw a woman standing there. He _____ her before.
　　［A］never saw　　［B］had never seen　　［C］never sees　　［D］has never seen
2. Some people think that animal research is irrelevant _____ our health and that it can often produce misleading results.
　　［A］with　　　　［B］at　　　　　［C］on　　　　　［D］to
3. When asked by the police, he said that he remembered _____ at the party, but not _____.
　　［A］to arrive; leaving　　　　　　　　［B］to arrive; to leave
　　［C］arriving; leaving　　　　　　　　［D］arriving; to leave

4. Among the four candidates, superior educational background and overseas study experience make Linda different from _____ .

   [A] everyone else　[B] the other　[C] someone else　[D] the rest

5. _____ it with me and I'll see what I can do.

   [A] When left　[B] Leaving　[C] If you leave　[D] Leave

6. In my hometown, children are often _____ by parents to pay attention to their table manners during the Spring Festival.

   [A] demanded　[B] reminded　[C] allowed　[D] hoped

7. Ask your father for some money, _____ you will be unable to buy a bicycle before September.

   [A] or　[B] and　[C] then　[D] so

8. Rather than _____ on a crowded bus, he always prefers _____ a bicycle.

   [A] ride; ride　[B] riding; ride　[C] ride; to ride　[D] to ride; riding

9. Li Ming did not pass the exam, _____ .

   [A] so did Li Hua　[B] Li Hua did, too　[C] Li Hua didn't, too　[D] nor did John

10. —How long _____ each other before they _____ married?

    —For about a year.

    [A] have they known; get　[B] did they know; were going to get
    [C] do they know; are going to get　[D] had they known; got

11. I am preparing for a speech. What topic _____ ?

    [A] do you think I should choose　[B] you think I should choose
    [C] do you think should I choose　[D] do you think I should have chosen

12. Up to now there have been many explanations _____ the cause of sleepwalking.

    [A] in view of　[B] in line with　[C] apart from　[D] as to

13. I have lost one of my gloves. I _____ it somewhere.

    [A] must drop　[B] must have dropped
    [C] must be dropping　[D] must have been dropped

14. As a foreigner who first came to China, Mike had a hard time making himself _____ .

    [A] understand　[B] understood
    [C] understanding　[D] being understood

15. Maggie has been fortunate to find a job she loves and, _____ , she gets well paid for it.

    [A] sooner or later　[B] what's more
    [C] as a result　[D] more or less

第二部分　完形填空

阅读下面短文，从短文后所给的四个选项（[A]、[B]、[C]、[D]）中选出能填入相应空白处的最佳选项，并在答题卡上将该项涂黑。

Villages in developing countries often lack many things: books, clean water and electricity. These shortages are 16 to see. But a 17 kind of shortage is not easy to see. That is a shortage of 18 . Many villages have no doctors, engineers or scientists. They have no one who knows 19 to treat unusual medical problems or design a new expert system. There's a way to ease these problems. They can do it with 20 . In the past few years, computer scientists around the world 21 what they call expert systems. An expert system is a 22 kind of computer program. In some 23 , it can take the place of a human expert. For example, an expert in 24 system can help 25 a sick person. A question appears on the computer screen, "Is the person hot?" You tell the computer 26 yes or no. The computer asks 27 questions. "Has the person lost any blood?" "Can the person move normally?" You   28 . The computer continues to ask questions 29 it has enough 30 to make a decision. Then it tells what 31 or other treatment is needed. In this way the expert system takes the place of a 32 . Another kind of expert system takes the place of an engineer. It   33 the flow of water in the river. It tells if a dam can be built 34 the river. It also tells   35 electricity can be produced. Still other kinds of expert systems help solve problems for farmers and owners of small businesses.

16. [A] difficult   [B] easy   [C] unable   [D] easier
17. [A] strange   [B] similar   [C] different   [D] difficult
18. [A] engineers   [B] computers   [C] doctors   [D] experts
19. [A] what   [B] how   [C] when   [D] where
20. [A] computers   [B] scientists   [C] experts   [D] nothing
21. [A] have known   [B] have discovered [C] have found   [D] have developed
22. [A] particular   [B] peculiar   [C] special   [D] specific
23. [A] situations   [B] countries   [C] areas   [D] time
24. [A] medical   [B] agricultural   [C] computer   [D] industrial
25. [A] care for   [B] see   [C] take care   [D] look
26. [A] neither   [B] either   [C] or   [D] both
27. [A] much   [B] many   [C] no more   [D] other
28. [A] hear   [B] listen   [C] know   [D] answer
29. [A] after   [B] when   [C] until   [D] as
30. [A] time   [B] message   [C] answer   [D] information
31. [A] doctor   [B] medicine   [C] service   [D] answer
32. [A] hospital   [B] doctor   [C] person   [D] nurse
33. [A] stops   [B] understands   [C] measures   [D] makes
34. [A] for   [B] in   [C] on   [D] by
35. [A] how many   [B] how much   [C] much   [D] many

第三部分 阅读理解

阅读下列短文，从每题所给的四个选项（[A]、[B]、[C]、[D]）中选出最佳选项，并在答题卡上将该项涂黑。

A

YANGON—Myanmar has officially accepted an offer of the United States to send humanitarian aid（人道主义援助）to the country's cyclone（飓风；暴风）victims, state radio reported Friday in a night broadcast.

Myanmar Deputy Foreign Minister U Kyaw Thu gave the assurance Friday, saying that the country is receiving such relief aid from any country without limit at this time according to its policy of dealing with the disaster, the report said.

Kyaw Thu denied rumors about Myanmar's turning down of such relief materials from Western countries but accept those from nations in good relations with Myanmar, saying that the country has never done so in this case.

Kyaw Thu said that well wishers abroad may make cash donation through Myanmar embassies（使馆）stationed there, while those who like to donate relief goods may present at the Yangon International Airport and seaports.

According to the report, the US relief aid would arrive in Yangon in days.

"A foreign ministry's statement said earlier on Friday that at this moment, the international community can best help the victims by donating emergency provisions such as medical supplies, food, cloth, electricity generator, and materials for emergency shelter or with financial assistance," adding that "Myanmar will wholeheartedly welcome such course of action."

"The government and the people of Myanmar are grateful to the friendly nations, the United Nations, international organizations, non-governmental organizations, private individuals and others for their sympathy and generosity." it said.

36. Which of the following is true?
   [A] The US relief aid was turned down at first and then accepted.
   [B] The US relief aid has been sent to the capital city of Myanmar.
   [C] There are rumors that Myanmar has turned down the US relief aid.
   [D] Myanmar will wholeheartedly welcome such course of action but the US relief aid.

37. We Chinese may denote money to help the country's cyclone victims through _____ .
   [A] Myanmar embassies in Beijing
   [B] the Yangon International Airport
   [C] the United Nations
   [D] the Yangon International seaports

38. What can the international community（组织）best help the victims in Myanmar?
   [A] Medical supplies.　　　　　　[B] Financial assistance.

[C] Electricity generator.　　　　　　[D] All of the above.

39. What is Myanmar's policy toward the aids from abroad?

[A] Myanmar prefers cash donation to relief goods.

[B] Myanmar only receives emergency provisions such as medical supplies, food, cloth, electricity generator, etc..

[C] Myanmar receives donation relief aid from any country without any limit.

[D] Myanmar prefers relief goods to cash donation.

40. The title that best expresses the idea of the passage is _____.

[A] How to Help Myanmar

[B] Myanmar Accepts US Humanitarian Aid Officially

[C] Myanmar Is Receiving Relief Aid from Any Country Without Limit

[D] The Government and the People of Myanmar Are Grateful

B

The Diet Zone: A Dangerous Place

Diet Coke, diet Pepsi, diet pills, no-fat diet, vegetable diet... We are surrounded by the word "diet" everywhere we look and listen. We have so easily been attracted by the promise and potential of diet products that we have stopped thinking about what diet products are doing to us. We are paying for products that harm us psychologically and physically.

Diet products significantly weaken us psychologically. On one level, we are not allowing our brain to admit that our weight problems lie not in actually losing the weight, but in controlling the consumption of fatty, high-calorie, unhealthy foods. Diet products allow us to jump over the thinking stage and go straight for the scale (秤) instead. All we have to do is to swallow or recognize the word "diet" in food labels.

On another level, diet products have greater psychological effects. Every time we have a zero-calorie drink, we are telling ourselves without our awareness that we don't have to work to get results. Diet products make people believe that gain comes without pain, and that life can be without resistance and struggle.

The danger of diet products lies not only in the psychological effects they have on us, but also in the physical harm that they cause. Diet foods can indirectly harm our bodies because consuming them instead of healthy foods means we are preventing our bodies from having basic nutrients (营养成分). Diet foods and diet pills contain zero calorie only because the diet industry has created chemicals to produce these wonder products. Diet products may not be nutritional, and the chemical that go into diet products are potentially dangerous.

Now that we are aware of the effects that diet products have on us, it is time to seriously think about buying them. Losing weight lies in the power of minds, not in the power of chemicals. Once we realize this, we will be much better able to resist diet products, and therefore prevent the psychological harm that comes from using them.

41. From Paragraph 1, we learn that _____.

   [A] diet products fail to bring out people's potential

   [B] people have difficulty in choosing diet products

   [C] diet products are misleading people

   [D] people are fed up with diet products

42. One psychological effect of diet products is that people tend to _____.

   [A] try out a variety of diet foods

   [B] hesitate before they enjoy diet foods

   [C] pay attention to their own eating habits

   [D] watch their weight rather than their diet

43. In Paragraph 3, "gain comes without pain" probably means _____.

   [A] losing weight is effortless   [B] it costs a lot to lose weight

   [C] diet products bring no pain   [D] diet products are free from calories

44. Diet products indirectly harm people physically because such products _____.

   [A] are over-consumed   [B] lack basic nutrients

   [C] are short of chemicals   [D] provide too much energy

45. Which of the following shows the structure of the passage?

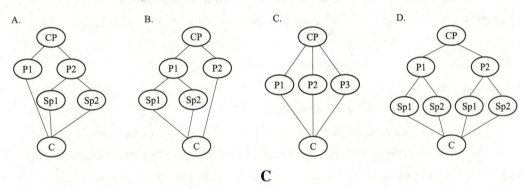

C

Tilly Smith, an 11-year-old British girl, who was called "Angel of the Beach," saved 100 tourists from a Thai beach hit by a tsunami on Dec. 26, 2004 and had been named "Child of the Year 2005" by readers of a French children's newspaper.

Tilly Smith is a schoolgirl at Danes Hill school in Oxshott, Surrey, England. Back from Thailand she told her geography class how the sea slowly rose and started to foam（起泡沫）, bubble, and form whirlpools（旋涡）before the big waves came.

"What Tilly Smith described as happening was exactly the same as I'd shown on a video of a tsunami that hit the Hawaiian Islands in 1946," said Andrew F. Kearney, Tilly's geography teacher. "She saw the consequences of not acting when something strange happens." Kearney said topics for sixth-grade pupils include earthquakes and volcanoes.

"We covered tsunamis because they can be caused by earthquakes, volcanoes, or landslides," he added, "I've taught this particular course for at least 11 years."

Kearney uses audiovisual (视听教学的) teaching aids such as interactive whiteboards to exploit geographic information online (his class often visits nationalgeographic.com). Tilly's class had looked up U. S. websites about tsunami's early warning systems.

"The teacher has a computer on the desk and can project different web pages onto the whiteboard," Kearney said, "It's helped make great strides in teaching geography, <u>it</u> really brings it into the classroom."

On December 26, 2004, Tilly Smith, ten, saw "bubbles on the water and foam sizzling (发出嘶嘶声) just like in a frying pan" while walking on Phuket Island beach with her family. Her mind kept going back to the geography lesson Mr. Kearney gave just two weeks before she flew out to Thailand on vacation. She recognized these as the warning signs of a tsunami.

She told her parents and alerted the staff of the Marriott hotel, where they were staying. The beach was evacuated (撤离) just minutes before the killer tsunami struck. It was one of the few on Phuket Island where no one was killed or seriously hurt.

46. The purpose of the passage is to tell us _____.
    [A] how geography is taught in British schools
    [B] how Tilly Smith used her knowledge to save tourists from tsunami
    [C] why Tilly Smith was named "Child of the Year 2005"
    [D] the relationship between classroom knowledge and its practical use

47. Which of the following words can best describe geography teaching in Britain?
    [A] Practical.   [B] Exciting.   [C] Audiovisual.   [D] Interactive.

48. The underlined word "it" in paragraph 6 refers to _____.
    [A] web page   [B] computer   [C] whiteboard   [D] geography

49. What can we learn from the last two paragraphs?
    [A] Tilly Smith's parents and the hotel staff had no knowledge of tsunamis.
    [B] No other beaches on Phuket Island were evacuated before the tsunami struck.
    [C] The warning signs of the tsunami were the same as Tilly Smith had learned.
    [D] Tilly Smith and her family had not left the hotel room before the tsunami struck.

D

What time is it? Most people are pretty accurate in their answer. And if you don't know for sure, it's very likely that you can find out. There may be a watch on your wrist; there may be a clock on the wall, desk, or computer screen; or maybe you're riding in a car that has a clock in the dashboard (仪表板).

Even if you don't have a timepiece of some sort nearby, your body keeps its own beat. Humans have an internal clock that regulates (调节) the beating of our heart, the pace of our breathing, the discharge (排出) of chemicals within our bloodstream, and many other bodily functions.

Time is something from which we can't escape. Even if we ignore it, it's still going by, ticking away, second by second, minute by minute, hour by hour. So the main issue in using your time well is, "Who's in charge?" We can allow time to slip by and let it be our enemy. Or we can take control of it and make it our ally.

By taking control of how you spend your time, you'll increase your chances of becoming a more successful student. Perhaps more importantly, the better you are at managing the time you devote to your studies, the more time you will have to spend on your outside interests.

The aim of time management is not to schedule every moment so we become all slaves of a timetable that governs every waking moment of the day. Instead, the aim is to permit us to make informed choices as to how we use our time. Rather than letting the day go by, largely without our awareness, what we are going to discuss next can make us better able to control time for our own purposes.

50. The underlined word "ally" in Para. 3 most likely means somebody or something that is _____.

    [A] your slave and serves you

    [B] your supporter and helps you

    [C] under your control and obeys you

    [D] under your influence and follows you

51. The author intends to tell us that time _____.

    [A] could be regulated by a timepiece such as a clock or a watch

    [B] could be managed by the internal clock of human bodies

    [C] should be well managed for our own interest

    [D] should be saved for outside interests

52. In the next part, the author would most probably discuss with you _____.

    [A] how to keep up with the times   [B] how to make up for lost time

    [C] how to have a good time   [D] how to make good use of time

E

For years we have been told that encouraging a child's self-respect is important to his or her success in life. But child experts are now learning that too much praise can lead to the opposite effect. Praise-sholic kids who expect it at every turn may become teens who seek to same kind of approval from friends when asked if they want to go in the backseat of the car.

The implication of saying "You are the prettiest girl in class," or talking about the goals she succeeded but not her overall effort, is that you love her only when she looks the best, scores the highest, achieves the most. And this carries over to the classroom.

Social psychologist Carrol Dweck, PhD, tested the effects of over praise on 400 fifth graders while she was at Columbia University. She found that kids praised for "trying hard" did better on tests and were more likely to take on difficult assignments than those praised for being "smart."

"Praising attributes（品质）or abilities makes a false promise that success will come to you because you have that quality, and it devalues effort, so children are afraid to take on challenges." says Dweck, now at Stanford University, "They figure they're better quit while they're ahead."

53. The underlined words "Praise-sholic kids" refers to kids who are _____.
   [A] tired of being praised   [B] worthy of being praised
   [C] very proud of being praised   [D] extremely fond of being praised

54. The author quoted（引用）Dr. Dweck's words in the last paragraph in order to make the article _____.
   [A] better-known   [B] better-organized   [C] more persuasive   [D] more interesting

55. We can infer from the passage that _____.
   [A] praise for efforts should be more encouraged
   [B] praise for results works better than praise for efforts
   [C] praising a child's achievements benefits his or her success in life
   [D] praising a child's abilities encourages him or her to take on challenges

第四部分　写　作

第一节　短文改错

此题要求改正所给短文中的错误。对标有题号的每一行做出判断：如无错误，在该行右边横线上画一个勾（√）；如有错误（每行只有一个错误），则按下列情况改正：

此行多一个词：把多余的词用斜线（\）划掉，在该行右边横线上写出该词，并也用斜线划掉。

此行缺一个词：在缺词处加一个漏字符号（∧），在该行右边横线上写出该加的词。

此行错一个词：在错的词下画一横线，在该行右边横线上写出改正后的词。

注意：原行没有错的不要改。

John put the last of paint in his model spaceship.	56. _____
He'd painted it silver and blue. He help it up to show Dad.	57. _____
"It looks greatly," said Dad, "Let me help you hang it."	58. _____
They hanged the model from the ceiling with thin thread.	59. _____
John watched the spaceship swing back or forth. He began to	60. _____
think about journeying all lonely out of space. "Suppose a man	61. _____
is in the spaceship," John said, "And could he run out of water to drink?"	62. _____
"Yes," said Dad, "And could he run out of air to breath?" "Of course."	63. _____
answered Dad. "Then which would happen to him?" John asked.	64. _____
"I don't think he'd live long. Do you think that?" asked Dad.	65. _____
"No, I don't think I'd like to be out in a spaceship." said John.	

第二节　书面表达

假定你是李明，前不久在英文报纸上读到一篇有关农村儿童辍学的报道。给该报社编辑写一封信，谈论一下农村儿童辍学的主要原因以及你的看法。

要点如下：

1. 辍学原因；
2. 家庭贫困是主要原因；
3. 看法：每个孩子都应有受教育的机会，愿将自己的零花钱送给失学儿童。

参考词汇如下：

编辑：editor

农村：countryside

儿童辍学：leaves school at an early age

零花钱：pocket money

注意：词数 100 个左右。

参考答案及解析

第一部分　单项填空

1. B【解析】题干中第一个句子所用的时态是一般过去时，而第二个句子中的动作应该发生在第一句中的动作之前，根据"过去的过去"对应过去完成时的原则，本题应该用 had never seen，故选 B。

2. D【解析】be relevant to 是一个固定搭配，意为"与……有关的"，介词要用 to。irrelevant 是 relevant 加上否定前缀 ir-构成的词语，意为"无关的"，它的用法与 relevant 相同，故选 D。

3. C【解析】remember to do sth. 意为"记得要做某事"，这件要做的事还没有发生；remember doing sth. 意为"记得做过某事"，这个事情已经发生。从题目的意思来看，"到达"与"离开"都已经发生了，所以这两个动词都应该用"v. +-ing"的形式。

4. D【解析】本题的意思是"在四个候选人中，Linda 以出色的教育背景和海外留学的经历而显得出众"。everyone else 意为"其他所有人"，the other 意为"另一个"，someone else 意为"其他某人"，the rest 意为"其余的人"。这里选择的范围被限制在四个候选人之内，所以用 the rest 最合适，故选 D。

5. D【解析】"祈使句+and+陈述句"的句型在英语考试中经常出现。本题的意思是"把这事交给我，我看看怎么办"。

6. A【解析】demand 意为"要求"，remind 意为"提醒"，allow 意为"允许"，hope 意为"希望"。本题的意思是"在我的家乡，家长们通常要求孩子在春节期间注意饭桌礼仪"。这里我们要取"要求"的意思，故选 A。

7. A【解析】or 意为"否则"，and 意为"而且，并且"，then 意为"那么，因而"，so 意为"因而，那么"。本题的意思是"问你父亲要些钱，否则你就不能在 9 月份前买自行车了。"故选 A。

8. C【解析】本题考查 prefer 和 rather than 的用法。prefer 后要用那个动词的不定式形式，而 rather than 后要用不带 to 的不定式。因此，本题中空白处应该分别填入 ride 和 to ride。

9. D【解析】本题考查 nor 的用法。A 和 C 两个选项如果单独使用，就没有问题。如果放入空白处，句子就出现了两套主谓结构，它们既没有用分号隔开，也没有并列连词，就出现了语法错误。B 项错在意思与句子要求不符。只有选项 D 不存在上述问题，因此是正确答案。实际上，nor 引导的倒装句可以放在一个完整的句子后面，而无须用分号或连接词连接。

10. D【解析】两人已经结婚，那么 marry 就应该用一般过去时，而结婚之前发生的事应该用过去完成时。因此，第一个空格处应该填入 had they known，第二个空白处应该填入 got。

11. A【解析】do you think 是一个插入语，这个短语本身已经用了疑问语气，所以句子里的其他主谓结构不必再用疑问语气。这样一来，我们就只需在 A 和 D 两项中来选择："should+have+过去分词"的结构表示"该做某事而没有做"的意思，由于演讲还没有发生，所以 do you think I should have chosen 用在这里就不合适了。因此，空白处应该是 do you think I should choose。

12. D【解析】in view of 意为"考虑到，由于"，in line with 意为"符合"，apart from 意为"除……之外"，as to 意为"关于，至于"。本句的意思是"到目前为止，我们有许多关于梦游的讨论。"故选 D。

13. B【解析】从第一句来看，"我"的手套已经丢失，那么情态动词应该选择 must，动词 drop 应该用一般过去时。综合这两方面的考虑，我们填入空白处的应该是 must have dropped，表示对过去事实的肯定性推测。

14. B【解析】本题考查宾补的用法。Mike 是让自己为人理解，因此要用动词的过去分词作宾补，故选 B。

15. B【解析】Maggie 找到了一份自己喜爱的工作，她薪水不错与这一点是递进关系。sooner or later 表示时间关系，what's more 表示递进关系，as a result 表示因果关系，more or less 表示程度，故选 B。

第二部分　完形填空

16. B【解析】本题选项中的四个词放回原文都不存在语法错误，因此不能单纯从选项提供的信息来选出正确答案。紧接这句话后，转折连词 but 连接了一个与本题紧密相关的句子。这句子使用了 not easy to see 这个词组，那么本题就应该选择 easy 这个词，才能与后面这句话形成转折关系。

17. C【解析】strange 意为"奇怪的，陌生的"，similar 意为"相似的"，different 意为"不同的"，difficult 意为"困难的"。本段开头列举了一些"短缺"的例子，后面又对另一类"短缺"的例子进行了说明，所以我们应该选择 different 这一项。

18. D【解析】本题要考生判断这种短缺是什么。后面列举了短缺的包括医生、工程师和科学家。选项 A 和 C 都只是其中一种，不能入选，否则，我们就会犯以偏概全的错误。然而，这些人都可以归入 experts 一类，所以 experts 可以入选。而且，我们可以从后面多处出现的 experts 判断出它的确是短缺的"对象"。至于 computers，这是解决短缺的途径，而不是短缺的内容。

19. B【解析】"what to do"结构中，what 是 do 的宾语，而本句中 treat 已经有宾语，所以不能用 what。how，when，where 都可以填入空白而不会引起语法错误。但是，从意思上来看，这些村落面临的困难是"没有人懂得如何医治疑难杂症或设计专门的系统"，所以我们应该选择表示方式的 how。

20. A 【解析】本题考查考生对上下文意思的把握能力。scientists 和 experts 都是这些村落缺少的，所以不能用他们来解决问题。我们把 nothing 放回原文的意思是"他们将无计可施"，但后面紧接着就讲述了如何用计算机来解决这些问题，所以这个选项也不正确，从文章后来的叙述来看，computers 正是解决专家短缺问题的途径。

21. D 【解析】我们可以把这题同下一题结合起来作答。从下一题知道，"计算机科学家们……被他们称作专家系统的东西"。know 意为"知道"，其对象是已经存在的事物。discover 意为"发现"，其对象也是已经存在的事物。find 意为"发现，找到"，其对象仍然是已经存在的事物。develop 意为"开发，发展"，暗示"从无到有"创造出某个事物。由此可见，科学家们是新发明了专家系统，所以 develop 为最佳选项。

22. C 【解析】本题考查了近义词的辨析。particular 意为"独有的，挑剔的"，侧重不同于普遍性的个性或特殊性。peculiar 意为"独特的，罕见的"，强调特有性，常与 to 连用。special 意为"特别的，专门的"，指人或物可以明辨的独有的特性，强调独有性。specific 意为"特定的，具体的"，着重指某事物具有的特定属性。这句话的意思是"专家系统是一种特殊的电脑程序"，强调了这种独有性，因此，本题的正确选项是 C。

23. A 【解析】situation 意为"情形，情况"，本题的意思是"在某些情形下，专家系统可以取代专家"。本文并没有分国家、地区和时间来介绍专家系统的作用，因此，本题的正确选项为 A。

24. A 【解析】medical 意为"医疗的，医学的"，agricultural 意为"农业的"，industrial 意为"工业的"。本句中有 a sick person 这个短语，由此我们可以推断出本题谈论的是一个医疗系统，应该选择 medical 这个词。

25. A 【解析】care for 意为"关怀，照顾"，take care 意为"当心"，后接介词 of 可表示"照顾"之意。本题的意思是"帮助照顾病人"。因此，正确答案是 care for。

26. B 【解析】本题考查了固定搭配。neither...nor..."既不……也不……"；either...or..."二者择一，要么……要么……"；both...and..."两者都"。根据句意，B 为正确选项。

27. D 【解析】在这句话之前，作者已经提出了计算机可能问的问题，那么这里的意思就是"计算机也会问其他问题"，所以 other 是合适的选项。

28. D 【解析】计算机"问"，那么人就应该是"答"，因此，本题的正确选项是 D。前面，作者提到对于 Is the person hot 这样的问题，我们要 tell the computer either yes or no，可见，我们不能"一听了之"。

29. C 【解析】计算机问问题发生在"有足够的信息"之前，并且到"有足够的信息"为止，所以我们应该用 until。

30. D 【解析】本题所选择的词语，要能作为 make a decision 的基础，因此 A 项可以排除。message 意为"消息，讯息"，用在这里意思不对。answer 是可数名词，如果要选择 C 项，必须用复数。因此，能填入文中空白处的就只有 information 这个词语。

31. B 【解析】计算机系统诊断的结果应该是"开药"和提供"治疗方案"，所以第一个空白处应该填入 medicine。由于计算机系统已经替代了医生的功能，所以我们现在不再需要 doctor。service 这个词用在医院提供的服务上不太合适。medicine 正好与 treatment 对应，因此，本题的正确选项是 B。

32. B【解析】计算机系统取代的是医生，而不是医院或护士，因此，本题的正确答案为 B。

33. C【解析】stop 意为"阻止"，understand 意为"理解"，measure 意为"测量"，make 意为"制造，安排"。这四个词中，与"水流量"搭配比较合适的是 measure 这个词，也与水利工程师的工作相关。

34. C【解析】由于水坝是修筑在河上的，所以要用 on the river。in the river 是"在河里"的意思，by the river 是"在河边"的意思。

35. B【解析】electricity 是不可数名词，我们因此可以排除 A 和 D 两个选项。从意思上来看，how much 比 much 更符合题意。

第三部分　阅读理解

A

36. C【解析】细节题。本文第三段首句 Kyaw Thu denied rumors about Myanmar's turning down of such relief materials from Western countries 可知。选项 B 根据文章 According to the report, the US relief aid would arrive in Yangon in days. 一句可以排除。

37. A【解析】细节题。本题可以从第四段首句 "Kyaw Thu said that well wishers abroad may make cash donation（现金捐助）through Myanmar embassies（使馆）stationed there..."确定本答案。

38. D【解析】细节题。可以从倒数第二段找出答案。

39. C【解析】细节题。答案可以从第二段和倒数第二段找出正确答案。

40. B【解析】主旨题。从新闻的首段可以找出本题答案。其他选项均为新闻的细节。

B

41. C【解析】推断题。从第一段可看出，人们很容易受到节食产品的吸引，就不去思考节食产品对人们身心健康的影响，于是花钱买那些产品。这些产品误导了人们。

42. D【解析】推断题。从第二段可看出，人们非常重视他们的体重，不加任何思考地去购买节食产品，只看是否有节食标签。这说明他们急于去尝试那些产品。

43. A【解析】细节题。从第三段可看出，每次我们喝下标明不含热量的饮料，就给我们一个暗示，我们不会增加体重，减肥是很容易的事（we don't have to work to get results.）。另外，本段的最后半句（and that life can be without resistance and struggle.）也说明了画线部分的意义。

44. B【解析】细节题。从第四段第二句可看出，吃所谓的节食食品，就是阻止人体吸收基本的营养成分。另外，从本段最后一句也可以看出，节食产品没有营养（Diet products may not be nutritional, and the chemical that go into diet products are potentially dangerous.）

45. B【解析】本题考查学生对文章结构的分析能力。文章从两个要点来说明中心观点，这两个要点是（1）节食产品对人们心理的伤害。（2）节食产品对人们身体的伤害。为了说明第一个要点，文章中用了两个自然段，即第二自然段和第三自然段（分析理解这里是正确回答此题的关键）。所以，答案选 B。

C

46. B【解析】主旨题。通读全文可知，文章重点介绍了 Tilly Smith 是如何利用课堂上所学知识拯救游客的。答案选 B。

47. A【解析】推理题。根据文章所介绍的英国小学的地理教学模式以及 Tilly Smith 所做的一切可以得出结论：英国的地理教学很实用。

48. B【解析】代词替代题。根据前文"The teacher has a computer on the desk and can project different web pages onto the whiteboard"可知，该句的意思应该是：它（计算机）把地理真实地带入了课堂。

49. C【解析】推理题。从文章倒数第二段的介绍可以得到答案，Tilly Smith 正是运用了地理课堂上学到的知识在海啸中救人。文章倒数第二段中"Her mind kept going back to the geography lesson..."也验证了这一点。B 项与原文信息不符；A、D 两项缺乏信息支持。

D

50. B【解析】猜测词义题。根据前面一个句子中 let it be our enemy 和 make it our ally 对比，与 enemy 对应的意思是 B 项。

51. C【解析】推理判断题。由第二段可以推断出作者想告诉我们的是：人体内的生物钟可以调节时间。

52. D【解析】推理判断题。根据文章最后一句："...what we are going to discuss next can make us better able to control time..."可以推断下一段作者将讨论人们如何充分利用时间。

E

53. D【解析】词义猜测题。从前文"...too much praise can lead to the opposite effect. Praise-sholic kids who expect it at every turn..."看，it 应该指 too much praise。

54. C【解析】推理判断题。从第四段引用 Dr. Dweck's 的话，让人看到这种表扬会导致孩子们退缩，害怕挑战，从而使文章更具说服力。

55. A【解析】推理判断题。从第三段"She found that kids praised for 'trying hard' did better on tests and were more likely to take on difficult assignments than those praised for being 'smart'."可以得知，答案选 A。

第四部分　写　　作

第一节　短文改错

56. in→on
57. √
58. greatly→great
59. hanged→hung
60. or→and
61. lonely→alone
62. the→a
63. breath→breathe
64. which→what
65. that→so

第二节 书面表达

Dear Editor,

In the countryside a lot of children are leaving school at an early age for various reasons. Some have to leave school because their families are too poor to pay for their education. Some find difficulties in study. Some have to help their parents to earn money. And some simply do not like studying. In my opinion the main reason that the children can not finish school is the poor living conditions of their families.

I think every child has the chance to receive education. As a student I can't do much about it. But I would like to give them all my pocket money and hope it will help some children.

Your sincerely,
Li Ming

Unit 4

Friendship

Part One Listening Practice

Section A

1. D   2. B   3. A   4. C   5. A

Section B

6. B   7. C   8. B   9. D   10. A

Section C

11) center   12) living room   13) comfortable
14) save the time   15) office hours

Section D

1) for dinner   2) That sounds fine   3) aren't you
4) be for you   5) I'm ready

Part Two Detailed Reading

译 文

真正的友谊

你是否曾好奇过那句名言"患难见真情"的精髓是什么呢?人们谈论友谊的真正价值,而实际上却不明白它到底代表着什么。

真正的友谊意味着人与人之间不必拘泥于繁文缛节。当你将朋友视若家庭一员,方达至真友谊的境界。在这种境界,即使不常写信,不常打电话,仍无碍于友谊长存。挚友之间不必为维系友情不变而常常见面。

挚友之间互相信任,以致一方落难,另一方毫不犹豫赴汤蹈火。友情坚固,挚友们甚至能战胜距离,天涯若比邻。在他们眼中,地域阻隔只不过是生活的一部分,这影响不了他们的友谊。真正的友谊永不会消逝。实际上,它会随着时光流逝而历久弥坚。真正的友谊因为彼此间的信任、鼓励与安慰愈发枝繁叶茂。当一人身陷烦恼,挚友仅仅听到电话里传来的一句"你好"就已了然于胸。甚至彼此沉默不语,他们都能心有灵犀。

当一人临难时,真正的朋友不会弃之不顾。他们会共同面对,相互扶持,甚至有损于另一方的利益亦在所不辞。真正的朋友不会彼此算计,他们不必如此。他们彼此认同对方的优点和缺点,襟怀坦诚,毫无隐瞒。他们不仅了解彼此的优势,也深谙彼此的劣势。他们互相尊重彼此的个性。事实上他们能够理解彼此的相似处,也能够尊重彼此的分歧点。真正的朋友不能容忍外人对他们的友谊指指点点。若是有人如此,他们会奋力反驳。

真正的朋友不是投机取巧的人。他们不会因有利可图而伸手帮忙。真正的友谊带着无私的标记。好友之间彼此扶持,即使全世界的人都反对他们。人生得知已挚友实在不易。若你仅获一位知已,请相信你已得上苍眷顾。请记得,所有的知交挚友都是朋友,但不是所有的朋友都能成为知交挚友。

Comprehension of the Text

1. C   2. D   3. A   4. D   5. C

Unit 4

 **Part Three Exercises**

Task 1

1. e	2. a	3. j	4. i	5. c
6. h	7. b	8. f	9. g	10. d

Task 2

1. via	2. horrifying	3. staff	4. cheered/cheer	5. declined
6. knocked down	7. splendid	8. colleagues	9. greeted	10. gone through

Task 3

1. They all <u>dressed up</u> to take part in the New Year's party.
2. You are always <u>welcome</u> to our house.
3. The local <u>authorities</u> decided to build a bridge over the river.
4. I have to <u>pick up</u> children from school.
5. She was <u>knocked down</u> by a bus.

Task 4

Yang Gang's Week Schedule for His Free Time

Sept. 13	2:00 a. m.	attend a Students' Union activity
Monday	7:30 p. m.	attend a lecture on American Literature
Sept. 14	2:00 p. m.	go to the library
Tuesday	7:00 p. m.	attend the class meeting
Sept. 15	4:00 p. m.	play basketball
Wednesday	7:00 p. m.	communicate with family online
Sept. 16	3:30 p. m.	visit Professor Wang
Thursday	7:00 p. m.	do math homework
Sept. 17	4:00 p. m.	take part in the basketball match
Friday	7:00 p. m.	see a film with classmates
Sept. 18	9:00 a. m.	visit Ming Tombs

Saturday	2:00 p. m.	visit the Great Wall
Sept. 19	9:00 a. m.	wash clothes
Sunday	3:00 p. m.	watch basketball games on TV

Part Four Supplementary Reading

译 文

笔 友

　　交笔友，也就是写信与其成为朋友，是很流行的交友方式。人们定期写信给对方，友谊就慢慢建立起来了。互联网诞生以前，在全世界各地，交笔友一直都很风行。笔友与网友差不多。一般来说，人们交笔友有的是为了了解不同地区的文化和生活方式，也有的是为了排遣寂寞。有些笔友定期写信给对方，在合适的时机也会见面；有些笔友通信的同时，也不时送礼物给对方，却一直只是通信联络，从不会面；而有些笔友彼此之间联络越来越少，最终音信全无，友谊也就此戛然而止。若你不知道如何交笔友，请继续往下读。

　　如何交笔友
　　交笔友最简单的方法是加入一个交笔友的俱乐部。全世界这类俱乐部非常多。在那里，我们可以根据个人的年龄、职业、好恶来找笔友，也可以去寻找一位与自己的文化背景截然不同的笔友。在交笔友的过程，我们能够开阔视野，品味异国风情。

　　为了省时省力，现在笔友们普遍通过互联网通信、寄电子卡片。这样不仅节省时间，而且便宜省力，交流也更即时快捷。如今笔友们不必再翘首等待对方邮寄过来的信件了。电子邮件是最新的交友方式。

　　交笔友的几点小建议
　　交笔友不要随意，最好根据个人的爱好、职业和文化背景谨慎选择。
　　不要留私人地址，可以使用邮局的邮箱号。
　　开始时不要透露私人信息，正面示人即可。
　　定期写信给他（她）。
　　初期不要答应与他（她）见面，要是实在等不及了，带个可靠的人一起去。
　　最初不要寄自己或家人的照片给他（她）。
　　不要透露个人财务特别是银行账户密码等信息。
　　要是觉得对方不投合，可以随时停止通信。

Unit 4

Comprehension of the Text

1. Mostly, pen friendship aims at learning other cultures, different lifestyles and to even get rid of loneliness.
2. The easiest way to make pen friends is to join a pen pal friendship club.
3. You can choose pen friends according to your hobbies, occupation and culture.

自我测试题

第一部分 单项填空

从［A］、［B］、［C］、［D］四个选项中，选出可以填入空白处的最佳选项，并在答题卡上将该项涂黑。

> **Example**：
> It is generally considered unwise to give a child _____ he or she wants.
> ［A］however ［B］whatever ［C］whichever ［D］whenever
> Answer：［A］［■］［C］［D］

1. I am going to _____ railway station, too. Can I give you _____ ride?
   ［A］the; a ［B］a; the ［C］/; a ［D］/; the
2. They thought the program was _____ investigating.
   ［A］worth ［B］worthy ［C］worthwhile ［D］worthing
3. In education, there should be a good balance among the branches of knowledge that contribute _____ effective thinking and wise judgment.
   ［A］at ［B］in ［C］for ［D］to
4. You are not allowed to park you car here. If you _____ it here, I will call the police.
   ［A］do park ［B］park ［C］parked ［D］have parked
5. —I feel much better now. —_____.
   ［A］Oh, that's very nice of you ［B］Congratulations
   ［C］It's a pleasure ［D］Oh, I'm glad to hear that
6. Listen to me, Tom. This company will pay _____ what your company can.
   ［A］almost twice as much as ［B］almost much twice as
   ［C］as almost twice much as ［D］as much as almost twice
7. Bill Clinton was the president of the United States from 1992 to 2000, _____ the US economy enjoyed a rapid growth.
   ［A］during which time ［B］for which time

[C] during whose time　　　　　[D] by that time

8. —A man came to say hello to me at the party, but I think we have never met before.
   —He must have taken you for _____.
   [A] some other　　[B] someone else　　[C] other person　　[D] one other

9. Tom, where did you put the _____ cups?
   [A] blue two coffee　[B] two blue coffee　[C] two coffee blue　[D] blue coffee two

10. Two men were sitting in a doctor's waiting room. "What are you in here _____?" asked one.
    [A] for　　[B] to　　[C] on　　[D] about

11. I haven't seen you since you came back from holiday. _____ a nice time?
    [A] Do you have　[B] Did you have　[C] Have you had　[D] Had you had

12. Li Ming will not come to our party, _____?
    [A] is he　　[B] do he　　[C] will he　　[D] won't he

13. Everybody is looking for you. You _____ home without a word.
    [A] mustn't leave　[B] shouldn't have left　[C] couldn't have left　[D] needn't leave

14. _____ I explained on the phone, your request will be considered at the next meeting.
    [A] When　　[B] After　　[C] As　　[D] Since

15. Liz won't be at work next week—_____ a well-earned break.
    [A] she has had　[B] she had　　[C] she was having　[D] she is having

第二部分　完形填空

阅读下面短文,从短文后所给的四个选项([A]、[B]、[C]、[D])中选出能填入相应空白处的最佳选项,并在答题卡上将该项涂黑。

The lecture on smoking was over at last. As we boys were rushing towards the playground, Jim slipped by the table. The watch, which Mrs. Smith had __16__ on the table as she started her lecture, disappeared.

We were __17__ to go back for class again when the headmaster called us __18__ and said, "I've got a little __19__ for you boys. Mrs. Smith has just lost her watch on the playground. This kind of thing has happened __20__, she says it just __21__ off her wrist (手腕). So, look around for it, will you? __22__ if you're clever enough to find it. Let's __23__ it clear the boys who does __24__ will get a useful reward (奖赏)."

At once we started looking for the watch. Everybody wished to be the __25__ one. Suddenly, Jim stopped and bent down as if to __26__ something. And __27__ he was in front of Mrs. Smith, all smiles, __28__ the watch to her.

Mrs. Smith, however, didn't seem at all __29__. In fact, she looked angry. She took the watch without __30__ a "Thank you."

Jim got __31__, a large piece of paper, from the headmaster, who __32__ him to write a composition __33__ the dangers of smoking. What could __34__ Jim write about? He hadn't listened to the lecture and had nothing to say on the __35__.

16. [A]	seen	[B]	dropped	[C]	found	[D]	laid
17. [A]	about	[B]	able	[C]	sorry	[D]	sure
18. [A]	forward	[B]	together	[C]	straight	[D]	out
19. [A]	fun	[B]	trick	[C]	job	[D]	prize
20. [A]	before	[B]	now	[C]	here	[D]	there
21. [A]	goes	[B]	throws	[C]	slips	[D]	falls
22. [A]	Say	[B]	See	[C]	Guess	[D]	Check
23. [A]	get	[B]	put	[C]	make	[D]	keep
24. [A]	this	[B]	such	[C]	that	[D]	so
25. [A]	lucky	[B]	quick	[C]	early	[D]	worthy
26. [A]	put down	[B]	give away	[C]	find out	[D]	pick up
27. [A]	the following moment			[B]	the next moment		
[C]	for a moment			[D]	just a moment		
28. [A]	handing out	[B]	turning in	[C]	giving up	[D]	sending back
29. [A]	pleased	[B]	hurt	[C]	interested	[D]	worried
30. [A]	just	[B]	ever	[C]	even	[D]	almost
31. [A]	her punishment	[B]	her prize	[C]	his job	[D]	his reward
32. [A]	had	[B]	made	[C]	told	[D]	helped
33. [A]	of	[B]	on	[C]	in	[D]	at
34. [A]	poor	[B]	nervous	[C]	quick	[D]	good
35. [A]	lecture	[B]	point	[C]	matter	[D]	subject

第三部分　阅 读 理 解

阅读下列短文，从每题所给的四个选项（[A]、[B]、[C]、[D]）中选出最佳选项，并在答题卡上将该项涂黑。

A

The largest earthquake (magnitude 里氏 9.5) of the 20th century happened on May 22, 1960 off the coast of South Central Chile.

It generated（生成）one of the most destructive Pacific-wide tsunamis（海啸）. Near the generating area, both the earthquake and the tsunami were very much destructive, particularly in the coastal area from Concepcion to the south end of Isla Chiloe. The largest tsunami damage occurred at Isla Chiloe—the coastal area closest to the epicenter（震中）. Huge tsunami waves measuring as high as 25 meters arrived within 10 to 15 minutes after the earthquake, killing at least two hundred people, sinking all the boats, and flooding half a kilometer inland.

There was large damage and loss of life at Concepcion, Chile's top industrial city. Near the city of Valdivia, the earthquake and following aftershocks generated landslides which killed 18 people. At the port city of Valparaiso, a city of 200,000, many buildings collapsed. A total of 130,000 houses were destroyed—one in every three in the earthquake zone and nearly 2,000,000 people were left homeless.

Total damage losses, including to agriculture and to industry, were estimated (估计) to be over a half billion dollars. The total number of death related with both the tsunami and the earthquake was never found accurately for the region. Estimates of deaths reached between 490 to 57,002 with no distinction (差别) as to how many deaths were caused by the earthquake and how many were caused by the tsunami. However, it is believed that most of the deaths in Chile were caused by the tsunami.

36. Where did the largest tsunami damage occur?
    [A] Concepcion.   [B] Isla Chiloe.   [C] Valdivia.   [D] Valparaiso.
37. What can we learn about the tsunami waves generated by the earthquake?
    [A] The tsunami waves as high as 25 meters arrived immediately after the earthquake.
    [B] The tsunami waves killed 200 people and sank all boats.
    [C] The tsunami waves were very destructive.
    [D] The tsunami waves flooded half of the inland.
38. What is generally thought the main cause of deaths in Chile?
    [A] Landslides.   [B] The tsunami.
    [C] Aftershocks.   [D] The magnitude 9.5 earthquake.
39. What is the total number of deaths in the earthquake?
    [A] 2,000,000.   [B] Between 490 and 57,002.
    [C] 200,000.   [D] It was hard to know.
40. What does the underlined word "collapsed" probably mean?
    [A] Were destroyed.   [B] Caught fire.
    [C] Were flooded.   [D] Sank.

B

Young adult filmmakers all hope to show their works in international festivals like Sundance and Toronto. But what about *really* young filmmakers who aren't in film school yet and aren't, strictly speaking, even adults?

They are at the heart of Wingspan Arts Kids Film Festival, tomorrow, in a setting any director might envy: Lincoln Center. Complete with "red carpet" interviews and various awards, the festival has much in common with events for more experienced moviemakers, except for the age of the participants: about 8 to 18.

"What's really exciting is that it's film for kids by kids." said Cori Gardner, managing director of Wingspan Arts, a nonprofit organization offering youth arts programs in the New York area. This year the festival will include films not only from Wingspan but also from other city organizations and one from a middle school in Arlington, Virginia. "We want to make this a national event." Ms. Gardner added.

The nine shorts to be shown range from a Claymation biography of B. B. King to a science fiction adventure set in the year 3005. "A lot of the material is really mature," Ms. Gardner said, talking about films by the New York City branch of Global Action Project, a media arts and leadership-training group. "*The Choice* is about the history of a family and *Master Anti-Smoker* is about the dangers of secondhand smoke." *Dream of the Invisibles* describes young immigrants' (移民) feelings of both belonging and not belonging in their adopted country.

The festival will end with an open reception at which other films will be shown. These include a music video and a full-length film whose title is *Pressures*.

41. Wingspan Arts Kids Film Festival _____.
    [A] is organized by a middle school
    [B] is as famous as the Toronto Festival
    [C] shows films made by children
    [D] offers awards to film school students

42. Which of the following is true of Wingspan Arts?
    [A] It helps young filmmakers to make money.
    [B] It provides arts projects for young people.
    [C] It's a media arts and leadership-training group.
    [D] It's a national organization for young people.

43. The underlined word "shorts" in Paragraph 4 refers to _____.
    [A] "short trousers"
    [B] "short kids"
    [C] "short films"
    [D] "short stories"

44. Movies to be shown in the festival _____.
    [A] cover different subjects
    [B] focus on kids' life
    [C] are produced by Global Action Project
    [D] are directed by Ms. Gardner

45. At the end of this film festival, there will be _____.
    [A] various awards
    [B] "red carpet" interviews
    [C] an open reception
    [D] a concert at Lincoln Center

C

The German port of Hamburg has been offered \$10,500 to change its name to "Veggieburg" by animal rights activists who are unhappy about the city's association with hamburgers. "Hamburg could improve animal welfare and bring kindness to animals by changing its name to Veggieburg." The People for the Ethical Treatment of Animals (PETA) wrote in a letter sent to Hamburg Mayor Ole Von Beust. The German branch of PETA, which has 750,000 members worldwide, said the organization would give Hamburg's childcare facilities 10,000 Euros worth of Vegetarian burgers if the city changed its name. But city officials in Hamburg, Germany's second largest city which traces its roots to the ninth century, were unmoved. "I cannot afford to waste my time with this. I don't even want to look at nonsense like this," said Klaus May, a city government spokesman, "But that doesn't mean we hamburgers don't have a sense of humor." In its letter, PETA said the name "Hamburg" reminded people of "unhealthy beef patties (肉饼) made of dead cattle." "Millions of people fall ill each year with deadly illnesses like heart disease, cancer, strokes and diabetes from eating hamburgers," PETA said in the letter.

The original "hamburger steak", a dish made of ground beef, traveled west with Germans to the United States in the 19th century. The first mention of "hamburgers" appeared on a menu in a New York restaurant in 1834. Some historians trace its beginning to a beef sandwich once popular with sailors in Hamburg. The city's name "Hamburg" comes from the old Saxon words "ham" (bay) and "burg" (castle). PETA recently made a similar offer to the U.S. town of Hamburg, New York. But their $15,000 bid was refused.

46. Why did PETA suggest changing the name "Hamburg"?
   [A] Because the name reminded people of a food made of animal meat.
   [B] Because changing the name can prevent people from eating hamburgers.
   [C] Because it can bring children much food to change the name.
   [D] Because hamburgers cause so many diseases every year.

47. What does the new name "Veggieburg" suggest?
   [A] Stopping eating meat.   [B] Eating vegetables instead of meat.
   [C] It's better for children to eat vegetables. [D] Treating animals better.

48. Which of the following statements of the German name "Hamburg" is true?
   [A] The name came from a kind of food.
   [B] The name came from the old German language.
   [C] The name has a long history.
   [D] The name has something to do with sailors.

49. What do you think is the result of the suggestion raised by PETA?
   [A] The two cities will have new names.
   [B] The present names of the two cities will last.
   [C] The children in Hamburg will have nothing to eat.
   [D] People won't eat hamburgers in the future.

D

It's killed at least two dozen people, damaged hundreds of homes, cost some 22 billion Yuan in direct economic losses so far and has left thousands of family-bound travelers stranded. The massive snow and ice storm that has swept through the southern part of China has put this country into full disaster management mode. Tens of thousands of soldiers have been activated and the government has already provided 126 million Yuan in aid to six provinces in the south slammed by the unexpected winter blast. But is enough being done? And what else can be done to ensure that the effects of natural disasters like the one in southern China are minimized in the future?

"Ni hao, you're listening to People In the Know, your window into the world around you, online at www.crienglish.com here on China Radio International. In this edition of the show, we'll be talking about the southern China snow and ice storm. So let's get started.

First, let's get a Chinese perspective of how well the ice and snow storm in southern China is being handled from a logistical point of view. For this we're joined on the line by Professor Peng Xizhe, Dean of the School of Social Development and Public Policy at Fudan University in Shanghai.

(Dialogue with Peng)

And after a short break, we'll talk about the broader view of disaster management."

"Ni hao, you're listening to People In the Know, your window into the world around you, online at www.crienglish.com here on China Radio International. I'm Paul James in Beijing. In this edition of the show, we're talking about the massive winter storm that has ravaged southern China. For a broader look at disaster management, we're joined on the line now by Mr. Aloysius Rego and Ms. Jiang Lingling, both with the Asian Disaster Preparedness Center in Thailand.

(Dialogue with Jiang and Rego)

And with that we close out this edition of People In the Know, online at www.crienglish.com here on China Radio International. Though it may seem small consolation now for the thousands who remain stranded because of the storm, it's important to remember that as long as patience prevails, you will get home. Questions or comments for us can be sent to crieng@crifm.com. For Executive Director Wang Lei and Producers Yang Jingjie and Xu Yang, I'm Paul James in Beijing. Take care."

50. What style does this passage belong to?

[A] An essay. [B] An Argumentation. [C] A description. [D] A news report.

51. What's the main idea of this article?

[A] Tell the stories about the snow storm in the southern part of China.

[B] Tell us some facts about the people in the disaster.

[C] What have been done or will be done to rescue the people in the disaster.

[D] Let's know the measures about the disaster.

52. How many people died from the snow disaster before this report?

[A] More than 30. [B] More than 24. [C] Many. [D] 50.

E

Beijing's broadened ban on smoking in public places took effect Thursday, adding force to the effort to hold a smoke-free Olympics.

The new rules extend existing anti-smoking regulations to more places, including fitness centers, cultural relic sites, offices, meeting rooms, dining halls, toilets and lifts. Restaurants, Internet cafes, parks, and waiting halls at airports, railway stations and coach stations are required to set up smoking areas. Hotels will have to offer smoke-free rooms or floors, but the regulations do not specify a proportion.

However, some restaurant owners have complained that it would be difficult to have a separate smoking room as required by the new regulations. "We plan to issue specific rules to solve this problem as soon as possible." Rao Yingsheng, vice-director of the Beijing Committee for Patriotic Public Health Campaign, was quoted by the Beijing News as saying Thursday. He said small restaurants without a separate room should set aside at least 70 percent of their area for non-smokers. He also said customers and restaurant owners would be asked for their thoughts on the new rule.

Local authorities dispatched about 100,000 inspectors to make sure the ban was being enforced Thursday. Everyone has the right to dissuade people from smoking in public places, Liu Zejun, who works for the Beijing committee, said. "Citizens are encouraged to expose those who refuse to obey the rule by calling the free telephone line 12320." Liu said.

People caught smoking in forbidden areas will be fined 10 Yuan ($1.40), while enterprises and institutions that violate (违反) the ban will face fines of between 1,000 Yuan and 5,000 Yuan. Smoking was forbidden in hospitals, kindergartens, schools, museums, sports venues and other places before the new regulations took effect. From Oct. 1 last year, the city also banned smoking in its 66,000 cabs, and imposed fines of 100 Yuan to 200 Yuan on drivers caught smoking in taxis.

China has pledged a cigarette-free, green Olympics. This year's event will be the first non-smoking Olympic Games since the Framework Convention on Tobacco Control (FCTC), of which China is a signatory (签名人), went into effect in 2005.

53. The passage mainly tells us _____.
   [A] there will be more places where smoking is forbidden.
   [B] more people should give up smoking.
   [C] broadened ban on smoking in public places took effect in order to set up a non-smoking Olympic Games.
   [D] those who smoke in public places will be fined.

54. Smoking is _____ at airports, railway stations or coach stations, etc.
   [A] forbidden   [B] allowed
   [C] allowed at it's smoking areas   [D] we don't know

55. Which of the following is NOT true according to the passage?
   [A] Hotels will have to offer smoke-free rooms.
   [B] Smoking is not allowed in most restaurants.
   [C] 12320 is a free telephone line to expose those who smoke at public places.
   [D] People caught smoking in forbidden areas will be fined.

第四部分　写　　作

第一节　短文改错

此题要求改正所给短文中的错误。对标有题号的每一行做出判断：如无错误，在该行右边横线上画一个勾（√）；如有错误（每行只有一个错误），则按下列情况改正：

此行多一个词：把多余的词用斜线（＼）划掉，在该行右边横线上写出该词，并也用斜线划掉。

此行缺一个词：在缺词处加一个漏字符号（∧），在该行右边横线上写出该加的词。

此行错一个词：在错的词下画一横线，在该行右边横线上写出改正后的词。

注意：原行没有错的不要改。

What is best way to learn a language? We should　　　　　　　　　56. _____

remember that we all learned our own language well　　　　　　　57. _____

when we are children. If we could learn a second language　　58. _____
in the same way, it would not seem such difficult.　　59. _____
Think of what little children do. They listen what people　　60. _____
say and try to imitate（模仿）what they hear. That　　61. _____
is important to remember that we learn our own language　　62. _____
with hearing people speak it. In school though you learn　　63. _____
to read and write as good as to hear and speak, it is　　64. _____
best to learn all new word through the ears.　　65. _____

第二节　书面表达

假定你是李明，会一点游泳，但水性不太好，想在国庆长假系统训练。某公司所登游泳训练广告称其有称职教练，一周包会。请用英语写一封信询问训练的具体情况。

要点如下：

1. 训练的具体时间和地点；
2. 所需条件及费用等。

参考词语：教练 instructor

注意：词数 100 个左右。

参考答案及解析

第一部分　单项填空

1. A【解析】railway station 是确定的事物，需要用定冠词 the。give someone a ride 是固定短语，意为"用车载某人一段路"，故选 A。

2. A【解析】be worth doing 是一个固定搭配，意为"值得做"。

3. D【解析】contribute 意为"起作用，有助于"，一般与介词 to 连用，故选 D。

4. A【解析】本题考查 do 构成强调句的用法。"do+动词原形"可以表示强调，并且 do 有人称和时态的变化。

5. D【解析】第一个人说感觉好一些了，可能是病情好转。那么，英文中得体的反应是对此表示欣慰，所以 I'm glad to hear that 是合适的选项。

6. A【解析】一般情况下，我们要用"倍数+as+形容词原级+as+比较对象"这一结构。四个选项中，只有选项 A 满足这一要求，故选 A。

7. A【解析】本题考查非限制性定语从句的用法。我们一般用 during 表示"在某个期间"，因此答案被锁定在 A 和 C 之间。这两个选项的区别在于 which 和 whose 的选择。由于这里指的是 1992 到 2000 年这段时间，没有所属关系的存在，所以要选择 which。

8. B【解析】someone else 意为"另外某个人"，而本题的意思是"他一定是把你当成另外某个人"，因此符合题意。

9. B【解析】在 two，blue，coffee 这三个词中，表示数量的词应该放在最前面，表示用途的放在最后面，因此，空白处应该填入的是 two blue coffee。

10. A【解析】空白处所在句子的意思是"你为什么来这里"，问的是目的。四个选项中只有 for 能用在这里表示目的，故选 A。

11. B【解析】本题考查时态。句意为"从你度假回来我就一直没有看见你。你玩得开心吗?"从前半句可知,假期是很久以前的事了,因此应该用过去时。

12. C【解析】本题考查附加疑问句的构成。由于主体部分用的是否定形式,助动词为 will,所以疑问部分用 will 的肯定形式,空白处应该填入 will he。

13. B【解析】mustn't 有"不许,绝对不可能"的意思,shouldn't have done 意为"本不该做某事(实际上做了)",couldn't have done 意为"不可能做了某事",needn't 意为"没有必要"。本题的意思是"大家都在找你,你不该话都不说一句就离开了"。因此,应该用 shouldn't have left。

14. C【解析】本句的意思是"就像我在电话里解释的那样,你的请求将在下次会议上讨论",故选 C。

15. D【解析】本题考查时态。此句表达的是将来的含义,A、B、C 都不符合,只有 D 为现在进行时表将来,故选 D。

第二部分　完形填空

16. D【解析】see 意为"看见",drop 意为"落下,下降",find 意为"发现,找到",lay 意为"放置"。Mrs. Smith 将表"放"在了桌上。因此,本题的正确选项是 D。

17. A【解析】be about to 是一个固定短语,一般与 when 搭配,意为"即将……的时候,……发生了"。本句的意思是"我们就要回教室上课的时候,校长把我们叫到了一起"。因此,本题的正确选项是 A。

18. B【解析】本句的意思是"校长把我们叫到了一起",应该用 together。因此,本题的正确选项是 B。

19. C【解析】从下文来看,校长是要大家找 Mrs. Smith 的手表,即分派给大家一个小"任务",应该用 job。

20. A【解析】本句的意思是"这种事情在以前也发生过",因此,本题的正确选项是 A。

21. C【解析】go 意为"离开,走开",throw 意为"扔,抛",slip 意为"滑动",fall 意为"倒下,跌倒"。本句的意思是"手表从她的手上滑落",应该用 slip。

22. B【解析】本句的意思是"看看你们够不够聪明,能不能找到它",所以要取"看"的意思,用 see。

23. C【解析】"make it+形容词+that 从句"是一个固定结构,it 作形式宾语,形容词作宾语补足语,that 引导的从句是真正的宾语。因此,本题的正确选项是 C。

24. D【解析】这个定语从句的意思是"做成这件事的孩子",这里的代词应该用 so。

25. A【解析】lucky 意为"幸运的",quick 意为"迅速的",early 意为"早的",worthy 意为"有价值的,可敬的"。由于找到手表有奖励,所以找到手表的孩子将是"幸运的"。因此,本题的正确选项是 A。

26. D【解析】put down 意为"放下,拒绝,镇压",give away 意为"分发,泛起,泄露,出卖",find out 意为"找出,发现",pick up 意为"捡起,获得,看到"。本题的意思是"Jim 弯下腰,好像是要捡起什么东西一样",对应的动作是 pick up。因此,本题的正确选项是 D。

27. B【解析】本句的意思是"Jim 捡起手表就站到了 Mrs. Smith 的面前"。for a moment 意为"片刻",just a moment 意为"稍等片刻",这两个短语在意思上与本句不符。在 the following

moment 与 the next moment 之间，后者更符合英语习惯。因此，本题的正确选项是 B。

28. B 【解析】hand out 意为"分发"，turn in 意为"上缴"，give up 意为"放弃"，send back 意为"退还"。从上下文来看，Jim 拿了 Mrs. Smith 的手表。他在这里假装找到了手表，然后主动交给了 Mrs. Smith，所以应该用 turn in。因此，本题的正确选项是 B。

29. A 【解析】pleased 意为"高兴的"，hurt 意为"疼的"，interested 意为"感兴趣的"，worried 意为"闷闷不乐的"。手表找到了，Mrs. Smith 本该高兴，不过这说明 Jim 偷了手表，所以她高兴不起来。因此，本题的正确选项是 A。

30. C 【解析】just 意为"仅仅"，ever 意为"曾经，在任何时候"，even 意为"甚至，连……都……"，almost 意为"几乎"。本句的意思是"她接过手表，甚至连句'谢谢'都没有说"。因此，本题的正确选项是 C。

31. D 【解析】上文中，校长曾经说找到手表的孩子将得到 a useful reward，现在 Jim 找到了，自然就要得到他的 reward。因此，本题的最佳选项是 D。

32. C 【解析】在四个选项中，只有 tell 能够使用 tell someone to do sth.，其他三个词一般都要接不带 to 的不定式。help 虽然有时也可以接带 to 的不定式，但是用在这里意思不合适。因此，本题的正确选项是 C。

33. B 【解析】本句的意思是"校长要 Jim 写一篇关于吸烟危害的文章"。能表示"关于"的介词有 on 和 about。因此，本题的正确选项是 B。

34. A 【解析】poor 意为"可怜的，贫穷的"，nervous 意为"紧张的，不安的"，quick 意为"快的"，good 意为"好的，优秀的"。Jim 找到了手表还受罚，而且又不会写受罚的作文，所以应该用"可怜"来形容他。

35. D 【解析】lecture 意为"演讲，讲座"，point 意为"要点，观点"，matter 意为"事件，问题"，subject 意为"题目，主题"。本文中，校长给了 Jim 一个"命题作文"，所以这里需用 subject。因此，本题的正确选项是 D。

第三部分 阅读理解

A

36. B 【解析】细节题。从文章第二段第三行"The largest tsunami damage occurred at Isla Chiloe—the coastal area closest to the epicenter（震中）."可以得到答案。

37. C 【解析】本题为细节题，考查文章第二段的最后几句。A 选项不是 arrived immediately 而是 10~15 分钟以后到来。B 选项为至少 200 人，D 选项不是 half of the inland 而是 half a kilometer inland，故以上 3 个选项均有误。

38. B 【解析】最后一段的最后一句"However, it is believed that most of the deaths in Chile were caused by the tsunami."说明本题答案。

39. D 【解析】细节题。2,000,000 为无家可归人的数目；200,000 为 the city of Valparaiso 的人口数。490 to 57,002 为地震和海啸共同导致的死亡数。

40. A 【解析】由本段的下一句"A total of 130,000 houses were destroyed..."可以推测出答案。

B

41. C 【解析】细节理解题。根据文章第一、二段可知，这次的电影节是专为未成年人而设置的。选项 A 根据文章第三段中"...said Cori Gardner, managing director of Wingspan Arts, a

nonprofit organization offering youth arts programs in the New York area."一句可以排除；选项 B 无法从文中得到这样的比对信息；选项 D 根据文章第一段中 "But what about *really* young filmmakers who aren't in film school yet and aren't, strictly speaking, even adults?" 可以排除。

42. B【解析】细节理解题。根据文章第三段 ". . . a nonprofit organization offering youth arts programs in the New York area." 一句可知。选项 A、C 属于无中生有，与本文无关；选项 D 扩大了文章本意，应该是 in the New York area，而不是 national organization。

43. C【解析】词义猜测题。

44. A【解析】综合推断题。根据文章倒数第二段可知，这些影片涵盖了不同题材。选项 B、C、D 均属内容错误。

45. C【解析】细节理解题。根据文章最后一段 "The festival will end with an open reception. . ." 一句可知 C 为答案。其他选项属于无关信息。

C

46. A【解析】细节理解题。德国城市汉堡因为与食物汉堡包名字相似，很容易让人联想到汉堡包所带来的负面影响，所以善待动物组织建议更名。

47. B【解析】词义推测题。结合全文，善待动物组织反对用动物肉做的汉堡包，Veggieburg 的词头与蔬菜（vegetable）相近，意思是"用蔬菜做的汉堡包"，即提倡吃蔬菜。本题应用构词法去推断词的含义。

48. C【解析】细节理解题。名字可追溯到九世纪，所以历史久远，由第一段第八行 ". . . which traces its roots to the ninth century. . ." 可知答案选 C。A、B、D 三项表述均错误。

49. B【解析】综合判断题。两个城市都继续用现在的名字，因为两个城市都拒绝了 PETA 要求更名的提议。文章有两处信息 "But city officials in Hamburg, Germany's second largest city which traces its roots to the ninth century, were unmoved." 及 "But their $15,000 bid was refused." 有提示。

D

50. D【解析】通读全文，很显然，这是一篇新闻报道。

51. C【解析】文章第一段最后两句说明了报道的主要内容。

52. B【解析】文章第一句话就说明了，at least two dozen 至少 24 人。

E

53. C【解析】见本文开头。

54. C【解析】文章第二段提到了一些地方应当建立吸烟的场所，那么在这些地方的非吸烟场所，肯定是不准吸烟的。

55. B【解析】文章第三段提到了在一些饭店单设吸烟的房间有困难，可见在饭店是准许吸烟的，但必须是在特定的地方。

第四部分　写　作

第一节　短文改错

56. best→the best

57. √

58. are→were

59. such→so

60. listen→listen to

61. That→It

62. learn→learned

63. with →by

64. good→ well

65. word→words

第二节　书面表达

Dear Sir (or Madam),

  I have read your advertisement in the newspaper. You mentioned that your instructors are fully qualified and you ensure that learners will be able to swim after one week's training. Although I can swim a little, I am not very confident in the water. So I am interested in taking part in the training course. Fortunately, I have a seven-day holiday from October 1 to October 7. I would like to know when and where the course will be given, and how much the seven-day course costs. Besides, is there anything special that should be prepared or does your company provide everything necessary?

  Looking forward to hearing from you soon.

Sincerely yours,
Li Ming

Key to Test Paper 1

Part I　Listening Comprehension

Section A

1. C   2. B   3. D   4. B   5. A

Typescripts of Listening Comprehension

Directions: This section is to test your ability to give proper answers to questions. There are 5 recorded questions in it. After each question, there is a pause. The questions will be spoken two times. When you hear a question, you should decide on the correct answer from the 4 choices marked A), B), C) and D) given in your test paper. Then you should mark the corresponding letter on the Answer Sheet with a single line through the centre.

  Example: You will hear: I wonder if you could give Mr. Wang a message for me?
    You will read: A) I'm not sure.   B) You're right.
          C) Yes, certainly.   D) That's interesting.

  From the question we learn that the speaker is asking the listener to leave a message. Therefore, **C)** **Yes, certainly** is the correct answer. You should mark C) on the Answer Sheet.

Now the tests will begin.
1. Hi, Mike. How did you like the film you saw last night?
2. What time is the next train to Boston?
3. I really enjoy light music. How about you?
4. You look so pale. Are you all right?
5. Good morning, sir. Can I help you?

Section B

6. C   7. D   8. B   9. A   10. D

Typescripts of Listening Comprehension

Directions: This section is to test your ability to understand short dialogues. There are 5 recorded dialogues in it. After each dialogue, there is a recorded question. The dialogues and questions will be spoken two times. When you hear a question, you should decide on the correct answer from the 4 choices marked A), B), C) and D) given in your test paper. Then you should mark the corresponding letter on the Answer Sheet with a single line through the centre.

6. M: Nancy, why were you late for class this morning?
   W: I missed the bus.
   Q: Why was Nancy late?

7. M: What time does the meeting start?
   W: At 8:30. We have 15 minutes to get there.
   Q: What time is it now?

8. W: Good afternoon. Welcome aboard.
   M: I've got seat A6. I hope it is by a window so that I can see the view.
   Q: Where does this conversation most probably take place?

9. M: What's in that big bag over there?
   W: I bought some potatoes, tomatoes and cabbages.
   Q: What did the woman buy?

10. M: May I speak to Jason Daniel, please?
    W: Sorry. Nobody by that name works here.
    Q: What can we learn from the woman's words?

Section C

11. result   12. other than   13. households   14. reflects   15. such as

Typescripts of Listening Comprehension

Directions: In this section you will hear a short recorded passage. The passage is printed in the test paper, but with some words or phrases missing. The passage will be read three times. During the second reading, you are required to put the missing words or phrases that you hear on the Answer Sheet in order of the numbered blanks. The third reading is for you to check your writing. Now the passages will begin.

Since World War II, especially in the last few decades of the 20th century, large groups of foreigners have come and settled in the United States. The (11 result) is that many Americans speak a foreign language at home. Today, one in seven Americans speaks a language (12 other than) English. Spanish is the leading foreign language spoken by 17 million Americans. All together, 31.8 million Americans speak 329 foreign languages in the (13 households). That means there is an increase of 34 percent in foreign language usage since 1980. Asian languages are used by 14 percent of foreign language speakers. That (14 reflects) the new wave of immigrants from Asian countries (15 such as) India, Japan, Korea and the Philippines. However, fewer European languages are heard in American families than before.

Part Ⅱ Vocabulary & Structure
Section A
16. B	17. A	18. C	19. A	20. C
21. D	22. B	23. B	24. C	25. D

Section B
26. had come	27. equipment	28. (should) sign	29. invitation	30. attractive
31. pleased	32. dangerously	33. improvement	34. understood	35. repairing

Part Ⅲ Reading Comprehension
Task 1
36. A	37. C	38. B	39. D	40. C

Task 2
41. D	42. A	43. D	44. C	45. D

Task 3
46. natural beauty	47. various tourist activities	48. nature lovers
49. water sports	50. over 1,000	

Task 4
51. Q H	52. D M	53. K I	54. G E	55. S C

Task 5
56. old salary level	57. be hired	58. a premium
59. lose	60. during regular hours	

Part Ⅳ Translation—English to Chinese
61. 繁忙的商业中心通常也是开设餐厅的好地方。
62. 尽管价格似乎较高，顾客们还是喜欢购买我们的产品。
63. 我不得不来和你商量一下，应该采取什么措施来对付这种局面。
64. 如果你们能够提供令人满意的售后服务，你们的产品在这里肯定会有广阔的市场。
65. A) 对我们有助的一种技术也可能对我们有害，认识到这一点是很重要的。我们可以通过控制这种新技术来避免这种情况的发生。正如一位专家所说："我们必须记住，只有明智地应用技术才会使我们走向成功。"
    B) 亲爱的顾客：
       在本月的通讯中，你会发现一个既有趣又实用的主题：园艺。
       的确，园林不仅美化家园还会提高它的价值。许多专家把园艺推荐为一种放松和减少压力的手段。四月份是开始设计一个新花园的好时节。

Part V Writing

Model Writing

March 24th, 2000

Dear Mr. John Brown,

  Thank you very much for your letter of March 12th. We formally invite you to our company so that we can discuss the details of our cooperation. If you accept our invitation, please inform me of your flight. I have arranged for Miss Li of my company to meet you at the airport. Wish you a pleasant journey.

  Best regards.

Sincerely yours,
×××

Unit 5

Romance

 Part One Listening Practice

Section A

1. A	2. A	3. A	4. B	5. B
6. A	7. A	8. B	9. A	10. B
11. B	12. B	13. B	14. B	15. A
16. B	17. B	18. A	19. A	20. A

Section B

Task 1

1) fond of 2) answer my question 3) come on
4) care for 5) expect

Task 2

6) May I help you 7) this Thursday 8) I'm really sorry for that
9) That's all right 10) Don't worry 11) That could be great
12) having brought you so much trouble 13) It doesn't matter

75

Part Two　Detailed Reading

译 文

天作之合

　　凯利·希尔德布兰德不必担心婚后要不要随夫姓。现在这个不重要了，因为今年10月份，这位20岁的姑娘要嫁给一个与她重名的男人。不仅仅是姓氏把他们连在了一起。20岁的佛州学生凯利·卡特里娜·希尔德布兰德要嫁给24岁的银行职员凯利·卡尔·希尔德布兰德。

　　他们计划邀请100位客人出席婚礼，见证他们结为夫妻的神圣时刻。"他就是我梦寐以求的白马王子，"谈起未婚夫，希尔德布兰德小姐说，"我对另一半有特定的要求，他不仅都符合，而且远远超乎我的想象。"

　　他们的浪漫故事始于网络。去年的一个晚上，百无聊赖之际，凯利小姐出于好奇，在流行的社交网——脸谱网上搜索看看是否有人和她重名。结果只有一个来自德克萨斯的男孩，凯利·希尔德布兰德符合，所以她就给他发了条信息。"她说：'嗨，咱俩同名，很酷吧！'"凯利先生回忆时说，"我当时觉得她很可爱。"虽然他也有些不安，"我想大概我们前世有缘吧。"

　　接下来的三个月里二人通过电邮来往。后来，他们不时地打电话，再后来每天都通电话，有时还会煲电话粥。几个月后，希尔德布兰德先生在佛州见到了与他重名的姑娘，便彻底坠入了爱河。"现在想来实在有趣，"聊到在网上第一次接触，他说，"我当时真是做梦也想不到后来我们会结婚。"

　　凯利小姐在发第一条消息的几个月后，也就是12月，在海滩上，她收到了藏在藏宝盒中的钻石求婚戒指。"我相信这完全是上天的安排，"她说，"上天的计划真是棒极了！"

　　自订婚后，他们的生活并不是事事顺遂，因为两个人重名出了些麻烦。有一次，他们乘坐游轮的浪漫之旅差点被迫取消，因为旅行社以为有人心不在焉输了两遍订票信息，就删了其中一条。

　　二人也不知道该怎么写结婚请柬，最后他们决定把各自的中名加上。希尔德布兰德小姐说他们不打算让未来的孩子承袭他们的名字。"不，"她谈到，"我们绝不会再给孩子们起名叫凯利了。"

Comprehension of the Text

1. C　　　　2. D　　　　3. D　　　　4. C　　　　5. A

Unit 5

 **Part Three Exercises**

Task 1

| 1. d | 2. g | 3. i | 4. c | 5. a |
| 6. e | 7. j | 8. f | 9. b | 10. h |

Task 2

1. timing   2. vow   3. confusion   4. cyberspace   5. deleted
6. occasional 7. encounter 8. engagement 9. recall   10. witnessed

Task 3

1. John <u>fell in love with</u> Lucy at first sight.
2. I admire her for her bravery <u>from head to heel</u>.
3. They are <u>planning out</u> a web site.
4. Once the design problem is solved, everything will be <u>plain sailing</u>.
5. Would you kindly <u>pass along</u> my advice to her?

Task 4

Oct. 30, 2010

Dear Prof. Peterson,

  I'm very sorry to tell you that I'm having a fever. I'm feeling so terrible that I am unable to attend your lectures today. So, I'm writing to ask for a sick leave of one day. I enclose a medical certificate from the doctor. I should appreciate it if you grant me the leave.

Yours faithfully,
Wang Min

Part Four Supplementary Reading

译 文

迟到的情书

一封 10 年前的情书在壁炉后面被发现,一对爱侣得以再相逢,最后喜结良缘。

周五,现年 42 岁的史蒂夫·史密斯和同岁的卡门·鲁兹佩雷斯在分开 16 年后,步入教堂举行了婚礼。

这对爱侣在他们 20 多岁的时候就相爱并订了婚。那时,卡门在英国留学。

但是相恋一年后,卡门不得不回到法国,二人便渐行渐远。

几年后,史蒂夫给她写了一封信,希望能再续前缘。不巧的是,卡门的妈妈收到信后把信放在了壁炉台上,信后来滑到了壁炉后面。

此后 10 年里信都没有被发现,直到修缮房子的工人把壁炉移开,这封信才得以重见天日。

仍然未婚的卡门,念念不忘前男友,终于收到了信。信上这样写道:

"希望你现在安好。我写这封信是想知道你结婚没有,是否还想念我?盼望你的回信,可以的话,请保持联系。"

史蒂夫现在是一家工厂的主管,他说:"我没有写太多,因为我猜想她已经结了婚。我没料到竟然过了 10 年才有回音。"

卡门说开始她实在太紧张了,因为这么多年过去了,所以她不敢打电话给他,最后她终于鼓起勇气拨通了电话。

不久他们在巴黎见了面。然后结了婚,时光距初恋之时已经过去了 17 年。

史蒂夫说:"重逢的场景宛如电影情节,我们穿越机场大厅,投入对方的怀中。"

我们再次相遇又再度坠入爱河。我们深情对望,不到 30 秒,便热吻起来。"

"现在我们结了婚,很欣慰的是,那封信最终完成了它的'使命'。"

卡门认为这场婚礼使他们令人称奇的爱情故事达到了高潮。现今她与史蒂夫一同住在德文郡。

她说:"我之前一直没有结婚,现在我终于嫁给了我一直爱着的人。"

Comprehension of the Text

1. 17 years.
2. It slipped down the back of the fireplace.
3. It was found when the fireplace was removed for renovations.

Unit 5

> 自我测试题

第一部分　单项填空

从 [A]、[B]、[C]、[D] 四个选项中，选出可以填入空白处的最佳选项，并在答题卡上将该项涂黑。

> **Example:**
> It is generally considered unwise to give a child _____ he or she wants.
> 　　[A] however　　　　[B] whatever　　　　[C] whichever　　　　[D] whenever
> **Answer:** [A] [■] [C] [D]

1. The temperature in _____ area will of course partly be determined by how far it is from _____ sea.
   [A] an; the　　　　[B] a; /　　　　[C] the; the　　　　[D] an; /

2. —Listen, Tom, I am not coming tonight.
   —But you _____!
   [A] promises　　　　[B] promised　　　　[C] will promise　　　　[D] had promised

3. We've interviewed several candidates but haven't found _____ fit for the job.
   [A] one　　　　[B] ones　　　　[C] it　　　　[D] them

4. —Would you mind opening the door for me, please?
   —_____
   [A] Well, that's all right.　　　　[B] Oh, with pleasure.
   [C] Thank you all the same.　　　　[D] Don't mention it.

5. It was there, the police believe, _____ she was able to activate the recorder she kept in her bag.
   [A] until　　　　[B] which　　　　[C] that　　　　[D] when

6. —Were you late for the class yesterday?
   —No. It was not yet half past eight _____ I arrived at school.
   [A] before　　　　[B] when　　　　[C] that　　　　[D] until

7. —I am sure David will be able to find the library.
   —He has a pretty good _____ of direction.
   [A] idea　　　　[B] feeling　　　　[C] experience　　　　[D] sense

8. —Sorry, am I in your way? I'll move.
   —_____
   [A] Oh, well done!　　　　[B] Well, that's my pleasure.
   [C] Go ahead.　　　　[D] Thank you for your kindness.

79

9. _____ is accepted that truth is relatively, and not absolutely true.
   [A] It   [B] That   [C] What   [D] That it
10. It is said that John Major didn't himself go to Oxford, _____ most of his ministers did.
   [A] after   [B] since   [C] while   [D] if
11. She _____ the train until it disappeared in the distance, with tears filled in her eyes.
   [A] saw   [B] watched   [C] noticed   [D] observed
12. On September 11, the United States was attacked by terrorists and the World Trade Towers crashed, from _____ effects many survivors are still suffering.
   [A] that   [B] whose   [C] those   [D] what
13. As gas is getting more and more expensive, many people are _____ public transportation.
   [A] looking for [B] setting up   [C] turning to   [D] changing into
14. _____ me the keys—you're in no fit state to drive.
   [A] To give   [B] Giving   [C] Give   [D] Given
15. Professor Johnson will give a lecture on _____ the Roman Empire failed to conquer Asia.
   [A] why   [B] what   [C] who   [D] that

第二部分 完形填空

阅读下面短文,从短文后所给的四个选项([A]、[B]、[C]、[D])中选出能填入相应空白处的最佳选项,并在答题卡上将该项涂黑。

A couple of months ago, I went to a department store to buy a few things for the house. I __16__ a set of __17__ for the living room, two table lamps, a rug and several cushions. I asked them __18__ the things as __19__ as possible, but they said that they __20__ __21__ them out until 20 days __22__. After about 3 weeks, I __23__ only the curtains and table lamps. I was a little __24__ when I didn't receive all the items I had bought. But nevertheless, I am __25__ to see __26__ the curtains and lamps looked like. I first opened the package __27__ the curtain. I had bought a lovely light blue, and __28__ they had sent me a horrible dark purple. Well, you can __29__ imagine how __30__ I was. Then I opened the boxes with the lamps. They were exactly what I'd __31__. But one of the lamps shapes __32__. The next thing I did was to __33__ them to __34__. They promised to come to pick them up immediately and also to replace them with the correct order. It has been two weeks since my complaint. They have neither picked up the wrong items __35__ sent me the rest of my order.

16. [A] asked for   [B] needed   [C] took   [D] sent
17. [A] books   [B] curtains   [C] lamps   [D] tables
18. [A] to buy   [B] to sell   [C] to deliver   [D] to prepare
19. [A] much   [B] quick   [C] many   [D] soon
20. [A] were unable to [B] were able to   [C] were unwilling to [D] forgot to
21. [A] bring   [B] take   [C] send   [D] buy
22. [A] ago   [B] before   [C] later   [D] after

23. [A] sold	[B] accepted	[C] bought	[D] received
24. [A] disappointed	[B] happy	[C] worried	[D] nervous
25. [A] sorry	[B] angry	[C] eager	[D] sad
26. [A] what	[B] how	[C] that	[D] whether
27. [A] with	[B] for	[C] in	[D] outside
28. [A] instead	[B] then	[C] why	[D] so
29. [A] only	[B] just	[C] merely	[D] then
30. [A] happy	[B] angry	[C] tired	[D] kind
31. [A] sold	[B] asked	[C] bought	[D] ordered
32. [A] had damaged	[B] was damaged	[C] damaged	[D] was to damage
33. [A] ask	[B] go to	[C] telephone	[D] say to
34. [A] discuss	[B] change	[C] quarrel	[D] complain
35. [A] to	[B] or	[C] and	[D] nor

第三部分 阅 读 理 解

阅读下列短文，从每题所给的四个选项（[A]、[B]、[C]、[D]）中选出最佳选项，并在答题卡上将该项涂黑。

A

Federal regulators Wednesday approved a plan to create a nationwide emergency alert（警报）system using text messages delivered to cell phones.

Text messages have exploded in popularity in recent years, particularly among young people. The wireless industry's trade association, CTIA, estimate more than 48 billion text messages are sent each month.

The plan comes from the Warning Alert and Response Network Act, a 2006 federal law that requires improvement to the nation's emergency alert system. The act tasked the Federal Communications Commission (FCC) with coming up with new ways to alert the public about emergencies.

"The ability to deliver accurate and timely warnings and alerts through cell phones and other mobile services is an important next step in our efforts to help ensure that the American public has the information they need to take action to protect themselves and their families before, and during, disasters and other emergencies." FCC Chairman Kevin Martin said following approval of the plan.

Participation in the alert system by carriers—telecommunications companies—is voluntary, but it has received solid support from the wireless industry.

The program would be optional for cell phone users. They also may not be charged for receiving alerts.

There would be three different types of messages, according to the rules.

The first would be a national alert from the president, likely involving a terrorist attack or natural disaster. The second would involve "approaching threats," which could include natural disasters like hurricanes or storms or even university shootings. The third would be reserved for child abduction (绑架) emergencies, or so-called Amber Alerts.

The service could be in place by 2010.

36. What is the purpose of the approved plan?
   [A] To warn people of emergencies via messages.
   [B] To popularize the use of cell phones.
   [C] To estimate the monthly number of messages.
   [D] To promote the wireless industry.
37. The carriers' participation in the system is determined by _____.
   [A] the US federal government
   [B] mobile phone users
   [C] the carriers themselves
   [D] the law of the United States
38. Which of the following is true of cell phone users?
   [A] They must accept the alert service.
   [B] They may enjoy the alert service for free.
   [C] They must send the alerts to others.
   [D] They may choose the types of messages.
39. An alert message will NOT be sent if _____.
   [A] a child loses his way   [B] a university shooting happens
   [C] a natural disaster happens   [D] a terrorist attack occurs
40. Which of the following would be the best title for the text?
   [A] Cell Phone Alerts Protecting Students
   [B] Cell Phone Alerts by Wireless Industry
   [C] Cell Phone Alerts of Natural Disasters
   [D] Cell Phone Alerts Coming Soon

B

It was the summer of 1965. Deluca, then 17, visited Peter Buck, a family friend. Buck asked Deluca about his plans for the future. "I'm going to college, but I need a way to pay for it," Deluca recalls saying, "Buck said, 'You should open a sandwich ship.'"

That afternoon, they agreed to be partners. And they set a goal: to open 32 stores in ten years. After doing some research, Buck wrote a check for $1,000. Deluca rented a storefront (店面) in Connecticut, and when they couldn't cover their start-up costs, Buck kicked in another $1,000.

But business didn't go smoothly as they expected. Deluca says, "After six months, we were doing poorly, but we didn't know how badly, because we didn't have any financial controls." All he and Buck knew was that their sales were lower than their costs.

Deluca was managing the store and going to the University of Bridgeport at the same time. Buck was working at his day job as a nuclear physicist in New York. They'd meet Monday evenings and brainstorm ideas for keeping the business running. "We convinced ourselves to open a second store. We figured we could tell the public, 'We are so successful, we are opening a second store.'" And they did—in the spring of 1966. Still, it was a lot of learning by trial and error.

But the partners' learn-as-you-go approach turned out to be their greatest strength. Every Friday, Deluca would drive around and hand-deliver the checks to pay their suppliers. "It probably took me two and a half hours and it wasn't necessary, but as a result, the suppliers got to know me very well, and the personal relationships established really helped out," Deluca says.

And having a goal was also important. "There are so many problems that can get you down. You just have to keep working toward your goal," Deluca adds.

Deluca ended up founding Subway Sandwich, the multimillion-dollar restaurant chain.

41. Deluca opened the first sandwich shop in order to _____.
    [A] support his family   [B] pay for his college education
    [C] help his partner expand business   [D] do some research

42. Which of the following is true of Buck?
    [A] He put money into the sandwich business.
    [B] He was a professor of business administration.
    [C] He was studying at the University of Bridgeport.
    [D] He rented a storefront for Deluca.

43. What can we learn about their first shop?
    [A] It stood at an unfavorable place.
    [B] It lowered the prices to promote sales.
    [C] It made no profits due to poor management.
    [D] It lacked control over the quality of sandwiches.

44. They decided to open a second store because they _____.
    [A] had enough money to do it
    [B] had succeeded in their business
    [C] wished to meet the increasing demand of customers
    [D] wanted to make believe that they were successful

45. What contributes most to their success according to the author?
    [A] Learning by trial and error.   [B] Making friends with suppliers.
    [C] Finding a good partner.   [D] Opening chain stores.

C

Japanese doctors have used thin sheets of tissue from people's cheeks to repair damaged corneas (角膜). A team from Osaka University transplanted thin layers of cheek cells onto the eyes of four patients with a rare and painful eye condition, reports BBC online. Patients whose vision had been cloudy could see well afterwards, and the "new corneas" remained clear more than a year after the operation.

Doctors can also take cells from a healthy eye and grow them in a dish to produce a new cornea, or they can transplant corneas from donors. But these techniques may not work when both eyes are too badly damaged by accident or disease.

The team hopes their work may help solve the problem and lead to other types of grow-your-own tissue transplants. The cornea is the clear layer of cells on the surface of the eye. It can be damaged by trauma (外伤) or by a range of diseases.

The team worked with four patients who had a painful condition that caused cloudy corneas and dry eyes. Often the eye can regenerate cornea cells but none of the four patients had this ability. The researchers took a 3 mm-wide square of tissue from inside the mouth (cheeks) and grew it into a thin layer in the lab. They used a special low-temperature technique to separate a very think sheet off each batch (组). They then laid that onto the patient's eye. The cell layers stuck onto the eye and developed into tissue that looked and acted like a healthy cornea.

However, long-term follow-up and experience with a large series of patients are needed to assess the benefits and risks of this method. "Yet, it does offer the potential of treating severe eye diseases that are resistant to standard approaches." said the head of the research, Kohji Nishida.

46. Now doctors can repair the damaged corneas with the following methods except _____.
   [A] using mouth tissue
   [B] taking cells from a healthy eye and growing them in a dish
   [C] transplanting corneas from another person
   [D] using finger tissue

47. If both eyes are too badly damaged, we can treat them _____.
   [A] only by using mouth tissue
   [B] by taking cells from a healthy eye and growing them in a dish
   [C] by transplanting healthy corneas from donors
   [D] by none of the mentioned methods

48. We can infer from the passage that _____.
   [A] the new technique can be widely used in the operations
   [B] the new technique needs to be further tested
   [C] the new technique has more benefits than risks
   [D] any new technique has risks

49. Which of the following is the best title?
   [A] A New Invention   [B] A New Technique
   [C] Mouth Tissue Can Restore Your Vision   [D] Transplanting Can Restore Your Vision

D

Can trees talk? Yes—but not in words. Scientists have reasons to believe that trees do communicate with each other. Not long ago, researchers learned some surprising things. First a willow tree (柳树) attacked in the woods by caterpillars (毛毛虫) changed the chemistry of its leaves and made them taste so terrible that the caterpillars got tired of the leaves and stopped eating them. The even more astonishing, the tree sent out a special vapour—a signal causing its neighbors to change the chemistry of their own leaves and make them less tasty.

Communication, of course, doesn't need to be always in words. We can talk to each other by smiling, raising our shoulders and moving our hands. We know that birds and animals use a whole vocabulary of songs, sounds and movements. Bees dance their signals, flying in certain patterns that tell other bees where to find nectar (花蜜) for honey. So why shouldn't trees have ways of sending messages?

50. From the passage we know that caterpillars _____.
  [A] like willow trees   [B] enjoy eating fallen leaves
  [C] can talk to other caterpillars [D] can send out a special vapour
51. Caterpillars will stop eating willow tree leaves which _____.
  [A] have a chemical change and become tasteless
  [B] have a pleasant taste
  [C] are being attacked
  [D] are communicating
52. According to the passage, bees communicate with each other by _____.
  [A] talking   [B] making unusual sounds
  [C] singing songs   [D] flying certain patterns

E

Twenty years ago, I drove a taxi for a living. One night I went to pick up a passenger at 2:30 a.m. When I arrived to collect, I found the building was dark except for a single light in a ground floor window.

I walked to the door and knocked, "Just a minute." answered a weak, elderly voice.

After a long pause, the door opened. A small woman in her eighties stood before me. By her side was a small suitcase.

I took the suitcase to the car, and then returned to help the woman. She took my arm and we walked slowly toward the car.

She kept thanking me for my kindness. "It's nothing," I told her, "I just try to treat my passengers the way I would want my mother treated."

"Oh, you're such a good man," She said. When we got into the taxi, she gave me an address, and then asked, "Could you drive through downtown?"

"It's not the shortest way," I answered quickly.

"Oh, I'm in no hurry," she said, "I'm on my way to a hospice (临终医院). I don't have any family left. The doctor says I don't have very long."

I quietly reached over and shut off the meter (计价器).

For the next two hours, we drove through the city. She showed me the building where she had once worked, the neighborhood where she had lived, and the furniture shop that had once been a ballroom where she had gone dancing as a girl.

Sometimes she'd ask me to slow down in front of a particular building and would sit staring into the darkness, saying nothing.

At dawn, she suddenly said, "I'm tired. Let's go now."

We drove in silence to the address she had given me.

"How much do I owe you?" she asked.

"Nothing." I said.

"You have to make a living," she answered, "Oh, there are other passengers," I answered.

Almost without thinking, I bent and gave her a hug. She held onto me tightly. Our hug ended with her remark, "You gave an old woman a little moment of joy."

53. The old woman chose to ride through the city in order to _____.
   [A] show she was familiar with the city   [B] see some places for the last time
   [C] let the driver earn more money   [D] reach the destination on time

54. The taxi driver did not charge the old woman because he _____.
   [A] wanted to do her a favor   [B] shut off the meter by mistake
   [C] had received her payment in advance   [D] was in a hurry to take other passengers

55. What can we learn from the story?
   [A] Giving is always a pleasure.
   [B] People should respect each other.
   [C] An act of kindness can bring people great joy.
   [D] People should learn to appreciate others' concern.

第四部分　写　　作

第一节　短文改错

此题要求改正所给短文中的错误。对标有题号的每一行做出判断：如无错误，在该行右边横线上画一个勾（√）；如有错误（每行只有一个错误），则按下列情况改正：

此行多一个词：把多余的词用斜线（＼）划掉，在该行右边横线上写出该词，并也用斜线划掉。

此行缺一个词：在缺词处加一个漏字符号（∧），在该行右边横线上写出该加的词。

此行错一个词：在错的词下画一横线，在该行右边横线上写出改正后的词。

注意：原行没有错的不要改。

Early men did not have clocks. They were told time by the	56. _____
sun and shadows of trees. At first time, they used	57. _____
sticks placing in the ground instead of trees. They made	58. _____
marks in the ground, and the shadows from the sticks told	59. _____
the time of day. Later, men began to use sundials. Some of	60. _____

sundials were boxes which sticks cast a shadow. Men were able to take the sundial box with them. The mark for noon was very important. The sundials always have to face the same way or the time was wrong. Sundials were good only on sunny days, not on cloud days. They were the first kind of clock.

61. _____
62. _____
63. _____
64. _____
65. _____

第二节　书面表达

假定你是李明，现在在英国工作，你的朋友王华写信告诉你他打算赴英留学，想知道初到英国可能会遇到的困难。请你用英语给他写一封回信，信的内容应包括以下几个方面。

1. 可能会遇到的困难：语言方面的障碍、饮食的不习惯、想家、孤独等；
2. 鼓励他并表示愿意帮助他。

注意：词数 100 个左右。

参考答案及解析

第一部分　单项填空

1. C【解析】两个空白处对应的名词都需特指，所以空白处应填入 the。

2. B【解析】此题考查时态。

3. A【解析】C 和 D 选项都对应确定的人或物，而在这里不要求确指，所以我们可以首先排除这两项。本题的意思是"我们已经面试了几个候选人，但没有找到一个适合那份工作的人"。因此，one 用在这里更合适。

4. B【解析】本题考查情景会话。句意为"——你能为我打开一下门吗？——非常乐意。""非常乐意"即 with pleasure，这是习惯性用法，所以答案为 B。A 和 D 都是别人说感谢时自己说的"不用谢"，C 为别人帮自己没有起作用时答谢时说的。

5. C【解析】本句考查强调句的用法。the police believe 在句中作插入语，我们可以将其去掉再解题。本句的意思是"她正是在那里打开了包里的录音机"。强调句一般要用 that 来连接，故选 C。

6. B【解析】本题的意思是"我到学校的时候，还不到 8∶30"，根据句意正确答案是 B。

7. D【解析】方向感的英文表达是 the sense of direction，故选 D。

8. D【解析】本题考查情景会话。句意为"——对不起，我是不是挡住你了，我来挪一挪。——太感谢了！"四个选项中只有 D 符合语境，为答案。

9. A【解析】题目中真正的主语是由 that 引导的主语从句，由于这个句子过长，所以我们将其后置，而用 it 作形式主语。故选 A。

10. C【解析】这句话的意思是"其他大臣大多数都曾就读于牛津大学，而 John Major 自己却没有在那里上过大学"。两个分句间存在转折关系，因此我们需要一个能表示转折的连接词。四个选项中只有 while 有此用法，故选 C。

11. B【解析】see 意为"看见"，强调看的结果；watch 意为"注视，注意，看守"；notice 意为"注意到"；observe 意为"观察，观测，遵守"。本题的意思是"她注视着火车，直到它消失在远处，眼睛里充满了泪水"。因此，空白处应该填入 watched。

12. B【解析】本题考查非限制性定语从句引导词的选择。that 不能引导非限制性定语从句，我们遇到这类题目就应该首先将其排除。those 和 what 根本就不能引导定语从句，所以也要排除。剩下的 B 项就是正确答案，将 whose 代入题干，意思就是"在 9 月 11 日，美国遭受了恐怖袭击，世贸大楼垮塌了。许多生还者还在经受着这一事件的影响"。

13. C【解析】本题考查词组意义辨析。look for 意为"寻找"；set up 意为"建立"；turn to 意为"求助于，询问，转向"；change into 意为"把……变成，换（衣）"。句意为"因为油价越来越贵，所以很多人都开始乘坐公共交通工具"，故选 C。

14. C【解析】本题考查祈使句的用法。本句意思为"把钥匙给我，因为你不在开车的状态"。祈使句要使用动词原形，故选 C。

15. A【解析】本题考查宾语从句连接词的选择。宾语从句主谓宾齐全，所以连接词应在从句中作状语。四个选项中只有 why 能作原因状语，that 用在这里虽然不会引起语法上的错误，但不如 why 意思通顺。本题的意思是"Johnson 教授将举办一次关于罗马帝国为何未能征服亚洲的讲座"。

第二部分　完形填空

16. B【解析】ask for 意为"请求，寻找"，need 意为"需要"，take 意为"取，拿走"，send 意为"送，发送"。文中的意思是作者"需要"下述东西，因此，本题的正确选项是 B。

17. B【解析】要选出本题的正确答案，需要联系下文的内容。后面提到商店给他送去了 curtains 和 table lamps，所以他需要的东西里面也有这两样东西。table lamps 已经在清单里面，所以缺少的是 curtains。

18. C【解析】从后面作者收到商店送过来的商品这一事实来看，作者是要求商店送货上门。因此，填入空白处的应该是 to deliver。

19. D【解析】much 和 many 表示数量，quick 表示速度，soon 表示时间。本题的意思是"我请他们尽快送货"，指的是时间上"尽快"，因此填入空白处的应该是 soon。

20. A【解析】be unable to 意为"不能"，be able to 意为"可以，能够"，be unwilling to 意为"不愿意"，forget to 意为"忘记"。从文章的意思来看，商店并非不愿意早送，而是没有能力早送，因此最合适的短语是 be unable to。

21. C【解析】bring 意为"带来"，take 意为"带走，拿"，send 意为"送，发送"，buy 意为"购买"。商店是要给作者送货，因此，本题的正确选项是 C。

22. C【解析】ago 和 before 表示"……之前"，用在这里意思不对。after 要放在所修饰词的前面。只有 later 的意思和用法都正确。

23. D【解析】sell 意为"出售"，accept 意为"接受"，buy 意为"购买"，receive 意为"收到，接到"。由于作者收到了自己订购的帘子和台灯，我们应该用 receive。

24. A【解析】disappointed 意为"失望的"，happy 意为"高兴的"，worried 意为"担心的"，nervous 意为"紧张的，不安的"。作者没有收到自己订购的所有东西，其正常的反应是 disappointed。

25. C【解析】sorry 意为"遗憾的，抱歉的"，angry 意为"愤怒的，生气的"，eager 意为"热心的，渴望着的"，sad 意为"忧愁的，悲哀的"。这个时候，作者还没有打开包装看到自己买的东西，所以他应该是渴望看自己订购的东西怎么样。因此，最佳词语为 eager。

26. A【解析】look like 后面要接一个介词宾语才能使句子完整，因此我们选择的连接词必须能够在宾语从句中充当介词宾语。四个选项中只有 what 能有此语法功能，所以正确答案为 A。

27. A【解析】本句是想表达"装有帘子的包裹"，我们一般用 with 这个介词。考生即使不知道这个用法，也可以从后面的 "Then I opened the boxes with the lamps..." 这句话中推断出这里的空白处应该填入 with 这个词语。

28. A【解析】instead 意为"代替，改为"，then 意为"然后，那么"，why 意为"为什么"，so 意为"因此，因而"。作者订购的是浅蓝色的帘子，而收到的却是暗紫色的，所以这里应该用 instead 这个词。

29. B【解析】only 意为"仅仅，只不过"，just 意为"正好，仅仅"，merely 意为"仅仅，只"，then 意为"那么，因而"。这里，just 还可以表示"也许，可能，完全"的意思。从意思上看，只有将 just 放回原文比较贴切。

30. B【解析】作者收到的货物与自己订购的不符，心情当然不会太好，所以正确的选项是 B。

31. D【解析】sell 意为"卖"，ask 意为"问"，buy 意为"买"，order 意为"订购"。A 和 B 两项显然不对，本题的难点在于 buy 和 order 的选择。由于本次交易并非一手交钱一手交货，而是交货时间在三周后，所以用 order 更合适。

32. B【解析】由于台灯是被损坏的，所以应该用被动语态。同时，事情发生在过去，又应该用一般过去时。综合考虑，空白处应该填入 was damaged。

33. C【解析】从文中的意思来看，作者没有亲自跑到商店去理论，但又通过协商取得了对方换货和发送余下货物的承诺，因此很可能是给商店打了电话。因此，填入文中空白处的最佳词语是 telephone。

34. D【解析】discuss 意为"讨论"，change 意为"更换，替换"，quarrel 意为"争吵"，complain 意为"抱怨，控诉"。从上下文来看，作者是打电话到商店投诉了，因此填入文中空白处的最佳词语是 complain。

35. D【解析】neither...nor... 意为"既不……也不……；既没有……也没有……"，是固定搭配。

第三部分 阅读理解

A

36. A【解析】细节理解题。根据文章第一段 to create a nationwide emergency alert（警报）system using text messages delivered to cell phones 一句可知答案。选项 B、C、D 属于与本题无关的信息。

37. C【解析】细节理解题。根据文章第五段 "Participation in the alert system by carriers—telecommunications companies—is voluntary." 一句可知。

38. B【解析】细节理解题。根据文章 They also may not be charged for receiving alerts. 一句可知。选项 A、C、D 明显不正确。

39. A【解析】细节理解题,同时也是一道逆向思维的题目。根据文章倒数第二段列举了一些需要对公众进行警告的内容,可以进行排查。

40. D【解析】主旨大意题。文章第一段即是主旨所在。选项 A 缩小了文章内容表达的范围;选项 B 不是本文所要表达的中心内容,明显不正确;选项 C 太片面,根据文章倒数第二段中 a terrorist attack or natural disaster 一句可以排除。

B

41. B【解析】细节理解题。根据文章第一段"I'm going to college, but I need a way to pay for it,"一句可知。选项 A、C、D 明显不正确。

42. A【解析】细节理解题。根据文章 Buck wrote a check for $1,000 和 Buck kicked in another $1,000 两句可知答案。选项 B、D 明显不正确;选项 C 句子主语已经偷换,属于张冠李戴。

43. C【解析】细节理解题。根据文章第三段可知。选项 A 与文章无关;选项 B 属于错误信息;选项 D 内容不正确。

44. D【解析】细节理解题。根据文章第四段中"We figured we could tell the public, 'We are so successful, we are opening a second store.'"一句可知。选项 A、B、C 均不正确。

45. A【解析】细节理解题。本题问的是作者认为什么是最主要的原因,因此要在文中找到作者的相关评论,根据文章第四段最后一句"Still, it was a lot of learning by trial and error..."可知。

C

46. D【解析】前三项的方法都在文中有所提及,但 D 项没有。

47. D【解析】根据第一段和第二段提到的技术及第二段"But these techniques may not work when both eyes are too badly damaged by accident or disease."可知,these techniques 即是指本题中前三项的内容。

48. B【解析】由最后一段第一句可知。

49. C【解析】本文主要讲述的是利用嘴部组织来修复受损的眼角膜技术。

D

50. A【解析】判断题。正因为毛毛虫觉得柳树叶可口,它们才吃柳树叶的。

51. A【解析】语义理解题。从第 1 段第 5 句话"First a willow tree(柳树)attacked in the woods by caterpillars(毛毛虫)changed the chemistry of its leaves and made them taste so terrible that the caterpillars got tired of the leaves and stopped eating them."可以做出正确选择。

52. D【解析】语义理解题。从第 2 段倒数第 2 句话"...flying in certain patterns that tell other bees where to find nectar(花蜜)for honey"可以知道 bees 交流的方式。

E

53. B【解析】考查整体推断的能力。老人请求开车穿过市区(Could you drive through downtown?),然后,她说她要去临终医院(I'm on my way to a hospice.)。在接下来的两个小时,她在车上最后观看了市区的景象,回忆了她年轻时的情景。最后她到达了临终医院。

54. A 【解析】考查简单推断的能力。出租车司机听老人说家里没有亲人了，就关掉了计价器。

55. C 【解析】考查推断理解能力。出租车司机没有收老人任何费用，很善良，使得老人感到很欣慰。同时老人也善良，主动要付给出租车司机费用，也使得出租车司机很感动。

第四部分 写 作

第一节 短文改错

56. 去掉 were

57. 去掉 time

58. placing→placed

59. in→on

60. some of→some

61. sticks→stick to

62. take→carry

63. have→had

64. √

65. cloud→cloudy

第二节 书面表达

Dear Wang Hua,

  I'm glad to hear from you. You asked me about the difficulties you may meet with when you get here. Now, I'd like to tell you something about it.

  First, you may have the problem about the language. You may find it difficult to communicate with the natives, because many of them have a strong accent. Besides, you may not get used to the western food here. What's more, you may feel lonely and miss your family and friends, especially in the very beginning.

  However, you needn't worry about it. Several weeks later, you will get used to everything here and love the place, and I'll also try my best to help you.

  Best wishes!

Yours,
Li Ming

Unit 6

Money

 Part One Listening Practice

Section A

1. C 2. A 3. D 4. B 5. C

Section B

6. D 7. B 8. C 9. A 10. B

Section C

11) step 12) are looking for 13) your own money
14) develop 15) your services

Section D

1) do me a favor 2) some cash 3) How much
4) Here you are 5) You are welcome

Unit 6

Part Two　Detailed Reading

译　文

金钱能不能买到快乐?

科学研究表明那些说金钱买不到快乐的人错了。

只要我们施与他人,或者花钱做些增长见识、有益身心的活动,而不是一味地购物,金钱是可以买到快乐的。

为了要获知美国人的花钱习惯与他们的自我快乐感之间的关系,2008年,美国的几位专家做了三个实验。第一个实验覆盖全国,632位美国人被要求详细说明各自的收支情况,同时标明自己的快乐感等级。

专家们发现与更高的快乐感等级密切相关的有两项:一项是高的收入,另一项是常送他人礼物或者捐钱给慈善机构。虽然过去研究显示富人并不比穷人更快乐,但是2009年的一项新的研究发现富人确实比收入一般或低收入的人快乐些。

有人会说富裕确实让人更开心,或者这与捐出的钱数有关,又或者经常给别人钱或捐钱做善事的人本身个性就开朗大方。因此,专家们为了验证上述说法,单独做了下面两个实验。

在第二个小型实验中,16位职员在拿到年终奖金前后都被要求说明他们的快乐感等级。不论奖金有多少,那些把奖金更多地花在他人身上或者捐出去的人都显示出比花在自己身上的人更快乐。

最后,第三个实验的结果非常有趣。46个人参与了这项实验,效果显示那些被要求把很少的一笔钱(5美元或10美元)给别人的人,他们的快乐感比那些将这笔钱拿来自己花的人要更高。与上个实验一样,钱的多少与快乐感不相关。这个实验的结果暗示即使不是自愿把钱施与他人时,人们还是能感受到快乐,甚至给别人带来的益处甚微时也是如此。

近日,另一项研究金钱与快乐的关系的实验同样验证了这一点。2009年研究者们发现了证据,有力地证实了早先的实验结果。与此同时,他们还发现当花钱参与活动增长见识、放松身心比如度假,而不是购物时,人们也比较开心。不过,人们只有在活动有益身心时才感到满意,要不然的话就谈不上开心愉快了。

钱财确实可以买来快乐,只要我们常常施与他人。把这句话牢记在心吧。

Comprehension of the Text

1. C 2. D 3. D 4. C 5. A

Part Three Exercises

Task 1

1. j 2. d 3. h 4. a 5. g
6. b 7. c 8. e 9. f 10. i

Task 2

1. conducted 2. shed light on 3. correlate with 4. give away 5. suggests
6. set out 7. confirmed 8. previous 9. turned out 10. positive

Task 3

1. <u>It turned out that</u> she had known him when they were children.
2. Is it really necessary to <u>conduct</u> experiments on animals?
3. His research results <u>correlate with</u> yours.
4. What is most <u>likely</u> to happen?
5. Recent research <u>has shed light on</u> the causes of the disease.

Task 4 Writing

Model

Lecture on IT Industry
Topic: On the Trend of IT Industry
Lecturer: Prof. Johnson
Sponsor: Department of Computer Science
Time: 3:00 p.m. Tuesday, March 20th
Place: Lecture Hall of Teaching Building A

Unit 6

Part Four Supplementary Reading

译文

在校生如何理财?

对于学生们来说，在校读书时如何理财是个不小的挑战。然而有了下面的指导，你就可以一路无虞地在钱财方面负起责任。

到校前做好财务小预算

列出"收入"（助学贷款、校内打工的薪水、父母补贴等）有哪些；列出"支出"有哪些，何时需要这些"支出"。当得到一学期或一学年的"收入"和"支出"数据后，便可将每月的"收入"和"支出"计算出来。如果每月"收入"大于"支出"，就表示你的财务状况良好。

校内打工

要是做完财务小预算后，发现你需要一些其他的收入，可以考虑在校内打工。很多学生上学时会做兼职。而校内的一些工作岗位比校外的更适合学生做。

学生优惠

通常大学周边的饭馆、书店、电影院、旅行社、服装店还有其他的商店会给予当地的学生一些优惠。学生在出示其学生证，询问是否有优惠时，表现得不必太害羞。你会惊喜地发现，在很多地方都有省钱的机会。

多思多想

既然能考上大学，智商一定不低，所以大家开动大脑好好想想节省支出的方法还有哪些吧！可否买二手书来代替新书呢？可否去杂货店买些牛奶麦片之类的放在宿舍而不是总去较贵的学校餐厅吃饭呢？可否换一些便宜一点的菜吃呢？花时间将要用到钱的地方和花费的预算记在本子上，转动你聪明的大脑想想怎么可以在这些地方省钱吧。

尽量不要用信用卡

对很多人来说，使用信用卡可以救急，但是代价有时却很高。信用卡的债务积累速度很快，越来越多的学生因为在大学时透支了信用卡而陷入财务危机。所以除非绝对需要，否则尽量不要用信用卡。

很多学生希望通过大学生活学会独立自主，自己掌握自己的生活。然而学会管理好钱财是独立自主的第一步。早些稳健地开始理财，免得为钱财忧虑而使得大学生活丧失了很多乐趣。记住：好好理财，受益多多。

Comprehension of the Text

1. How to make good use of money as a student.
2. a. Make a Budget Before You Arrive
   b. Get a Campus Job
   c. Use Your Student Discount
   d. Think Creatively
   e. Try to Avoid Using Credit Cards
3. Answers vary from person to person.

自我测试题

第一部分 单项填空

从［A］、［B］、［C］、［D］四个选项中，选出可以填入空白处的最佳选项，并在答题卡上将该项涂黑。

Example：
　　It is generally considered unwise to give a child ＿＿＿＿ he or she wants.
　　［A］however　　　［B］whatever　　　［C］whichever　　　［D］whenever
Answer：［A］［■］［C］［D］

1. ＿＿＿＿ Mr. Li called today, but not ＿＿＿＿ Mr. Li who called yesterday.
   ［A］/; a　　［B］A; the　　［C］/; the　　［D］The; a
2. If we ＿＿＿＿ everything ready by now, we should be having a terrible time tomorrow.
   ［A］hadn't got　　［B］didn't get　　［C］wouldn't have got　　［D］wouldn't get
3. The effects of rapid travel ＿＿＿＿ the body are far more disturbing than we realize.
   ［A］on　　［B］in　　［C］for　　［D］to
4. He has impressed his employers considerably and ＿＿＿＿ he is soon to be promoted.
   ［A］eventually　　［B］yet　　［C］finally　　［D］accordingly
5. My mother always gets a bit ＿＿＿＿ if we don't arrive when we say we will.
   ［A］anxious　　［B］ashamed　　［C］weak　　［D］patient
6. Do you still remember the chicken farm ＿＿＿＿ we visited three months ago?
   ［A］where　　［B］when　　［C］that　　［D］what
7. ＿＿＿＿ and new way to reduce her pain and suffering from the terrible disease, the patient sought her doctor's help to end her life.
   ［A］Having given up hope of cure　　［B］With no hope for cure

[C] There being hope for cure [D] In the hope of cure

8. She was so angry at all _____ he was doing _____ she walked out without saying a word.

   [A] that; that [B] which; that [C] what; as [D] that; which

9. —How about a film tonight?
   —_____ I haven't been to the cinema for a long time.

   [A] Yes, thanks. [B] Why not? [C] No, go away. [D] It's a pity.

10. Usually, _____ care for children's _____.

    [A] woman writers; lives [B] women writer; life
    [C] women writers; life [D] women writer; lives

11. I didn't manage to work out the problem _____ the teacher had explained how.

    [A] until [B] unless [C] when [D] before

12. Is it the watch you want _____?

    [A] to have it repaired [B] to repair it
    [C] to have repaired [D] to have repaired it

13. We will not attack _____ we are attacked; if attacked, we will certainly counter-attack.

    [A] if [B] when [C] unless [D] even if

14. You may write to me or come to see me. _____ way will do.

    [A] All [B] Both [C] One [D] Either

15. Mary is at the stage _____ she can not wash herself yet.

    [A] that [B] which [C] what [D] where

第二部分 完形填空

阅读下面短文，从短文后所给的四个选项（[A]、[B]、[C]、[D]）中选出能填入相应空白处的最佳选项，并在答题卡上将该项涂黑。

John lived all alone because his wife had died. He had worked hard as a tailor all his life, but misfortune had left him penniless. He had __16__ sons, but they only had time to __17__ and eat dinner with their father once a week.

__18__ the old man grew weaker and weaker, and his sons came by to see him less and less. He often worried __19__ would become of him, until at last he thought of a plan.

The next morning he went to see his friend, the carpenter (木匠), and asked him to make a large __20__. Then the locksmith (锁匠), and asked him for an old __21__. Finally the glassblower (吹玻璃的人) for all the broken pieces of glass he __22__. The old man took the chest home, filled it to the __23__ with broken glass, locked up tight and put it beneath his __24__.

"What's in this chest?" his sons asked, looking under the table.

"Oh, nothing," the old man replied, "just some things I've been __25__." They kicked it and heard a rattling (咯咯作响声) inside. "It must be full of all the gold he's saved over the years." they __26__ to one another.

So they talked it over and realized they needed to __27__ the treasure. They decided to __28__ living with the old man, and __29__ they could look after him, too. So the first week the youngest moved in, the second week the middle and the third week the eldest. This __30__ for some time.

At last the old father died. The sons gave him a very __31__ funeral（葬礼）, for they knew there was a __32__ sitting beneath the kitchen table. When the __33__ was over, they hunted through the house until they found the key, and unlocked the chest. To their astonishment, they found nothing but broken glass. But they didn't give up, and the eldest son turned over the chest to make sure if there was something valuable __34__ among the broken glass. On the bottom he found an inscription（题词）__35__ : Honor Your Father And Mother.

16. [A] four　　　　　[B] two　　　　　[C] three　　　　　[D] five
17. [A] stand by　　　[B] pass by　　　　[C] go by　　　　　[D] stop by
18. [A] Gradually　　 [B] Clearly　　　　[C] Fortunately　　 [D] Hurriedly
19. [A] what　　　　　[B] that　　　　　 [C] how　　　　　　[D] which
20. [A] shelf　　　　　[B] table　　　　　[C] cupboard　　　 [D] chest
21. [A] chest　　　　　[B] lock　　　　　 [C] cover　　　　　[D] saying
22. [A] made　　　　　[B] broke　　　　　[C] bought　　　　 [D] had
23. [A] top　　　　　　[B] bottom　　　　[C] center　　　　 [D] inside
24. [A] bed　　　　　　[B] house　　　　 [C] kitchen table　 [D] yard
25. [A] making　　　　[B] keeping　　　　[C] saving　　　　 [D] using
26. [A] whispered　　 [B] reported　　　 [C] shouted　　　　[D] pointed
27. [A] find　　　　　[B] own　　　　　　[C] know　　　　　 [D] guard
28. [A] take chances　[B] take turns　　 [C] take measures　[D] take actions
29. [A] on the way　　[B] by the way　　 [C] that way　　　 [D] in the way
30. [A] went on　　　　[B] kept on　　　　[C] moved on　　　 [D] put on
31. [A] sad　　　　　　[B] deep　　　　　 [C] rich　　　　　 [D] nice
32. [A] old man　　　 [B] fortune　　　　[C] guest　　　　　[D] lock
33. [A] service　　　 [B] celebration　　[C] meal　　　　　 [D] crying
34. [A] mixed　　　　　[B] painted　　　 [C] hidden　　　　 [D] grown
35. [A] writing　　　 [B] reading　　　　[C] telling　　　　[D] speaking

第三部分　阅 读 理 解

阅读下列短文，从每题所给的四个选项（[A]、[B]、[C]、[D]）中选出最佳选项，并在答题卡上将该项涂黑。

A

It had been some time since Jack had seen the old man. College, career, and life itself got in the way. In fact, Jack moved clear across the country in pursuit of his dreams. There, in the rush of his busy life, Jack had little time to think about the past and often no time to spend with his wife and son. He was working on his future, and nothing could stop him.

Over the phone, his mother told him, "Mr. Belser died last night. The funeral is Wednesday." Memories flashed through his mind like an old newsreel as he sat quietly remembering his childhood days.

"Jack, did you hear me?"

"Oh, sorry, Mom. Yes, I heard you. It's been so long since I thought of him. I'm sorry, but I honestly thought he died years ago." Jack said.

"Well, he didn't forget you. Every time I saw him he'd ask how you were doing. He'd reminisce (回忆) about the many days you spent over 'his side of the fence' as he put it." Mom told him.

"I told that old house he lived in." Jack said.

"You know, Jack, after your father died, Mr. Belser stepped in to make sure you had a man's influence in your life." she said.

"He's the one who taught me carpentry. I wouldn't be in this business if it weren't for him. He spent a lot of time teaching me things he thought were important... Mom, I'll be there for the funeral." Jack said.

Busy as he was, he kept his word. Jack caught the next flight to his hometown. Mr. Belser's funeral was small and uneventful. He had no children of his own, and most of his relatives had passed away.

The night before they had to return home, Jack and his Mom stopped by to see the old house next door one more time, which was exactly as he remembered. Every step held memories. Every picture, every piece of furniture... Jack stopped suddenly.

"What's wrong, Jack?" his Mom asked.

"The box is gone." he said.

"What box?" Mom asked.

"There was a small gold box that he kept locked on top of his desk. I must have asked him a thousand times what was inside. All he'd ever tell me was 'the thing I value most'." Jack said.

It was gone. Everything about the house was exactly how Jack remembered it, except for the box, He figured someone from the Belser family had taken it.

"Now, I'll never know what was so valuable to him." Jack said sadly.

Returning to his office the next day, he found a package on his desk. The return address caught his attention.

"Mr. Harold Belser." it read.

Jack tore open the package. There inside was the gold box and an envelope. Jack's hands shook as he read the note inside.

"Upon my death, please forward this box and its contents to Jack Bennett. It's the thing I valued most in my life." A small key was taped to the letter. His heart racing, and tears filling his eyes, Jack carefully unlocked the box. There inside he found a beautiful gold pocket watch. Running his fingers slowly over the fine cover, he opened it.

Inside he found these words carved: "Jack, thanks for your time! Harold Belser."

"Oh, My God! This is the thing he valued most..."

Jack held the watch for a few minutes, then called his assistant and cleared his appointments for the next two days. "Why?" his assistant asked.

"I need some time to spend with my son." he said.

36. Why did Jack think Mr. Belser died years ago?

   [A] College and career prevented him from remembering Mr. Belser.
   [B] Jack was too busy with his business and family to think about Mr. Belser.
   [C] Jack was too busy realizing his dreams to think about Mr. Belser.
   [D] His present busy life washed away his childhood memories.

37. Jack's mother told him on the phone about Mr. Belser EXCEPT that _____.

   [A] Mr. Belser often asked how Jack was doing
   [B] Mr. Belser's funeral would take place on Wednesday
   [C] Mr. Belser had asked for Jack's mailing address
   [D] Mr. Belser had pleasant memories of their time together

38. Why did Belser send Jack his gold watch?

   [A] Because he was grateful for Jack's time with him.
   [B] Because he had no children or relatives.
   [C] Because he thought he had to keep his word.
   [D] Because Jack had always wanted it during his childhood.

39. Why did Jack say he needed some time to spend with his son?

   [A] He was very tired of his work and wanted to have a good rest.
   [B] He had promised to spare more time to stay with his son.
   [C] He had missed his son and his family for days.
   [D] He came to realize the importance of the time with his family.

40. Which of the following is the most suitable title for this passage?

   [A] The Good Old Times   [B] What He Valued Most
   [C] An Old Gold Watch   [D] The Lost Childhood Days

B

Some futurologists have assumed that the vast upsurge (剧增) of women in the workforce may portend a rejection of marriage. Many women, according to this hypothesis, would rather work than marry. The converse (反面) of this concern is that the prospects of becoming a multi-paycheck household could encourage marriage. In the past, only the earnings and financial prospects of the man counted in the marriage decision. Now, however, the earning ability of a woman can make her more attractive as a marriage partner. Data show that economic downturns tend to putting off marriage because the parties cannot afford to establish a family or are concerned about rainy days ahead. As the economy comes to life, the number of marriages also rises.

The increase in divorce rates follows to the increase in women working outside the home.

Yet, it may be wrong to jump to any simple cause-and-effect conclusions. The impact of a wife's work on divorce is no less cloudy than its impact on marriage decisions. The realization that she can be a good provider may increase the chances that a working wife will choose divorce over an unsatisfactory marriage. But the reverse is equally plausible (似是而非的). Tensions grounded in financial problems often play a key role in ending a marriage. By raising a family's standard of living, a working wife may strengthen her family's financial and emotional stability.

Psychological factors also should be considered. For example, a wife blocked from a career outside the home may feel caged in the house. On the one hand, She may view her only choice as seeking a divorce. On the other hand, if she can find fulfillment through work outside the home, work and marriage can go together to create a stronger and more stable union.

Also, a major part of women's inequality in marriage has been due to the fact that, in most cases, men have remained the main breadwinners. A working wife may rob a husband of being the master of the house. Depending upon how the couple reacts to these new conditions, it could create a stronger equal partnership or it could create new insecurities.

41. The word "portend" (Line 2, Para. 1) is closest in meaning to "_____."
    [A] defy   [B] signal   [C] suffer from   [D] result from
42. It is said in the passage that when the economy slides _____.
    [A] men would choose working women as their marriage partners
    [B] more women would get married to seek financial security
    [C] even working women would worry about their marriages
    [D] more people would prefer to remain single for the time being
43. If women find fulfillment through work outside the home, _____.
    [A] they are more likely to dominate their marriage partners
    [B] their husbands are expected to do more housework
    [C] their marriage ties can be strengthened
    [D] they tend to put their career before marriage
44. One reason why women with no career may seek a divorce is that _____.
    [A] they feel that they have been robbed of their freedom
    [B] they are afraid of being bossed around by their husbands
    [C] they feel that their partners fail to live up to their expectations
    [D] they tend to suspect their husbands' loyalty to their marriage
45. Which of the following statements can best summarize the author's view in the passage?
    [A] The stability of marriage and the divorce rate may reflect the economic situation of the country.
    [B] Even when economically independent, most women have to struggle for real equality in marriage.
    [C] In order to secure their marriage women should work outside the home and remain independent.
    [D] The impact of the growing female workforce on marriage varies from case to case.

C

Melissa Poe was 9 years old when she began a campaign for a cleaner environment by writing a letter to the then President Bush. Through her own efforts, her letter was reproduced on over 250 donated billboards (广告牌) across the country.

The response to her request for help was so huge that Poe established Kids For A Cleaner Environment (Kids F. A. C. E.) in 1989. There are now 300,000 members of Kids F. A. C. E. worldwide and it is the world's largest youth environmental organization.

Poe has also asked the National Park Service to carry out a "Children's Forest" project in every national park. In 1992, she was invited as one of only six children in the world to speak at the Earth Summit in Brazil as part of the Voices of the Future Program. In 1993, she was given a Caring Award for her efforts by the Caring Institute.

Since the organization started, Kids F. A. C. E. members have distributed and planted over 1 million trees! Ongoing tree-planting projects include Kid's Yards—the creation of backyard wildlife habitats (栖息地)—and now Kids F. A. C. E. is involved in the exciting Earth Odyssey, which is a great way to start helping.

"Starting the club turned out to be a way to help people get involved with the environment. Club members started doing things like recycling, picking up litter and planting trees as well as inviting other kids to join their club."

"We try to tell kids that it's not OK to be lazy," she explains. "You need to start being a responsible, environmentally friendly person now, right away, before you become a resource-sucking adult."

46. Kids F. A. C. E. is _____.

    [A] a program to help students with writing

    [B] a project of litter recycling

    [C] a campaign launched by President Bush

    [D] a club of environmental protection

47. What can we learn about Poe?

    [A] She was awarded a prize in Brazil.

    [B] She donated billboards across the country.

    [C] She got positive responses for her efforts.

    [D] She joined the National Park Service.

48. Kid's Yards is _____.

    [A] established in a national park   [B] started to protect wildlife

    [C] a wildlife-raising project   [D] an entertainment park for kids

49. Which of the following can be inferred from the text?

    [A] Adults are resource-sucking people.

    [B] Poe sought help from a youth organization.

    [C] Kids F. A. C. E. members are from the U. S.

[D] Kids are urged to save natural resources.

D

Are you sometimes a little tired and sleepy in the early afternoon? Many people feel this way after lunch. They may think that eating lunch is the cause of the sleepiness. Or, in summer, they may think it is the heat. However, the real reason lies inside their bodies. At that time—about eight hours after you wake up—your body temperature goes down. This is what makes you slow down and feel sleepy. Scientists have tested sleep habits in experiments where there was no night or day. The people in these experiments almost always followed a similar sleeping pattern. They slept for one long period and then for one short period about eight hours later.

In many parts of the world, people take naps in the middle of the day. This is especially true in warmer climates, where the heat makes work difficult in the early afternoon. Researchers are now saying that naps are good for everyone in any climate. A daily nap gives one a more rested body and mind and therefore is good for health in general. In countries where naps are traditional, people often suffer less from problem such as heart disease.

Many working people, unfortunately, have no time to take naps. Though doctors may advise taking naps, employers do not allow it! If you do have the chance, however, here are a few tips about making the most of your nap. Remember that the best time to take a nap is about eight hours after you get up. A short sleep too late in the day may only make you feel more tired and sleepy afterward. This can also happen if you sleep for too long. If you do not have enough time, try a short nap—even ten minutes of sleep can be helpful.

50. Why do people feel sleepy in the early afternoon according to the text?
    [A] They eat too much for lunch.
    [B] They sleep too little at night.
    [C] Their body temperature becomes lower.
    [D] The weather becomes a lot warmer.
51. If you get up at 6:30 a. m. , what is the best time for you to take a nap?
    [A] About 12:30 p. m.   [B] About 1:30 p. m.
    [C] About 2:30 p. m.   [D] About 3:30 p. m.
52. What would be the best title for the text?
    [A] Just for a Rest   [B] All for a Nap
    [C] A Special Sleep Pattern   [D] Taking Naps in Warmer Climate

E

China news, Beijing, Feb. 9—Housing price in China has always aroused heated discussions among property developers and ordinary Chinese. To many property developers and local government officials, housing price in China is still low compared with many developed countries. However, the average housing price in the United States is only 8,000 Yuan per square meter, while in China, it is even higher than in the United States. This shows that there are some bubbles

（泡沫）in Chinese real estate market, the International Finance News reported.

Although the average price of residential houses in the United States, after converted to Renminbi, is about 8,000 Yuan per square meter, the houses in the US are not sold in terms of building area, as most Chinese property developers do when they sell their houses. If US property developers sell their houses according to the building area, then the housing price will be even lower than 8,000 Yuan per square meter. In most big Chinese cities, such as Beijing, Shanghai, and Shenzhen, houses are sold at a price even higher than those in the US.

The high housing sales price in large cities in China proves that Chinese real estate market does have some bubbles. Moreover, Chinese houses can not be compared with houses in the US in terms of building quality, environment and supporting facilities. Further more, it should be noted that American people's average income is several dozen times higher than that of Chinese people. How can the Chinese afford to buy a house which is even more expensive than that sold in the US?

At the beginning of 2007, Chinese government issued a set of policies that aimed to benefit the public. Now in order to reduce the high housing prices, the government can regulate（控制）the real estate market by raising tax on property industry and controlling the release of loans and lands to property developers. At the same time, the government should allow people to build more houses through various fund-raising channels, such as funds collected from buyers or raised by working units. By applying these multiple means, it is expected that the high housing prices can be lowered.

53. Which of the following does NOT support the idea that the average housing price in China is even higher than in the United States?

　　[A] Chinese houses can not be compared with houses in the US in terms of building quality, environment and supporting facilities.

　　[B] American people's average income is several dozen times higher than that of Chinese people.

　　[C] The houses in the US are not sold in terms of building area, as most Chinese property developers do when they sell their houses.

　　[D] There are more people who need houses in China.

54. What is the main idea of this passage?

　　[A] The housing price in China is so high that the government should do something useful to prevent it.

　　[B] There are some bubbles in Chinese real estate market.

　　[C] The average housing price in China is even higher than in the United States.

　　[D] Chinese government issued a set of policies that aimed to benefit the public.

55. How many measures are mentioned in the last paragraph in order to reduce the high housing prices?

　　[A] Two.　　　　　　[B] Three.　　　　　　[C] Four.　　　　　　[D] Five.

Unit 6

第四部分 写 作

第一节 短文改错

此题要求改正所给短文中的错误。对标有题号的每一行做出判断：如无错误，在该行右边横线上画一个勾（√）；如有错误（每行只有一个错误），则按下列情况改正：

此行多一个词：把多余的词用斜线（\）划掉，在该行右边横线上写出该词，并也用斜线划掉。

此行缺一个词：在缺词处加一个漏字符号（∧），在该行右边横线上写出该加的词。

此行错一个词：在错的词下画一横线，在该行右边横线上写出改正后的词。

注意：原行没有错的不要改。

Once there lived a scholar. Although he was as　　　　56. _____
poor as a church mouse, he was afraid for losing　　　　57. _____
face. One night the thief broke into his house,　　　　58. _____
but could find nothing worth of stealing. The　　　　59. _____
thief murmured, "What a bad luck!　　　　60. _____
I've run into a rich man's house!"　　　　61. _____
Heard this, the scholar quickly took a few coins　　　　62. _____
from his pocket what he had managed to save, and then　　　　63. _____
run after the thief. When he caught up with the thief,　　　　64. _____
he whispered, "Just took away these coins. Please　　　　65. _____
don't let anyone know about my poverty... don't let me lose face!"

第二节 书面表达

假定你是李明，想在BBS上发布一个英语帖子，讨论一下当今淡水资源缺乏的问题。要点如下：

1. 人们认为淡水是取之不尽的；
2. 当今淡水资源缺乏的实际情况；
3. 我们应该怎么做。

注意：词数100个左右。

参考答案及解析

第一部分 单项填空

1. B【解析】题干句子的意思是"一个李先生今天打过电话，但不是昨天打电话来的那个李先生"。因为说话人不知道第一个李先生是谁，因此不是确指，要用不定冠词a/an。第二个李先生是昨天打电话来的那个，因而是确指，要用定冠词the。

2. A【解析】本题考查虚拟语气的用法。本句的意思是"如果我们没有做好充分的准备，那么我们明天就得过艰难的日子了。"这只是一种假设的情况，故选A。

3. A【解析】本句的主语是the effects，谓语是are，far more disturbing than we realize可以整

体看作是表语。句子的意思是"迅速旅行给身体造成的影响远比我们以为的要令人不安得多。"因此，空白处所对应的短语是要补充说明 effects 的。effect 通常与 on 搭配使用，故选 A。

4. D【解析】eventually 意为"最后，终于"，yet 意为"然而，但是"，finally 意为"最后，终于"，accordingly 意为"因此"。本句的意思是"他给老板留下了非常好的印象，因此他很快升职了。"故选 D。

5. A【解析】本题要从句子意思来确定选项。anxious 意为"担忧的"，ashamed 意为"惭愧的，羞耻的"，weak 意为"虚弱的"，patient 意为"耐心的"。本句的意思是"如果我们说要来却还没有到达，那母亲的反应一般是担心、怕出事。"故选［A］。

6. C【解析】本题空白处及以后的句子为定语从句修饰先行词 farm。定语从句中的 visit 是一个及物动词，后面要接宾语，所以我们要选一个能作宾语的引导词。只有选项 C 中的 that 能在定语从句中充当宾语，故选 C。

7. B【解析】从"病人寻求医生帮助结束生命"来看，病人已经无治愈希望，选项 C 和 D 的意思与此矛盾，所以首先排除。A 项可单独作状语，但关键是这里 and 后面还有一个短语。如果用了 A，那么 no way to reduce her pain and suffering from the terrible disease 就在语法上有毛病。如果将 B 填入空白，那么 no way to reduce her pain and suffering from the terrible disease 可以作 with 的介词宾语，就不会存在语法上的问题了。故选［B］。

8. A【解析】前一个 that 引导定语从句修饰 all，后一个 that 引导结果状语从句。

9. B【解析】根据句意，应是：好啊，因为很长时间没有去看电影了，故选 B。

10. C【解析】本题考查名词复数，故选 C。

11. A【解析】本题考查词组 not... until..."直到……才……"。

12. C【解析】have sth. done=have sth. to be done "使某种东西被……"。
    例：I have my broken watch repaired. =I have my broken watch to be repaired. 我把我的手表拿去修了。

13. C【解析】根据句意，应选 unless "除非"。

14. D【解析】本题考查不定代词的用法，故选 D。

15. D【解析】本题考查定语从句的用法。此句的先行词为 at the stage，表示一个地点，因此选择 where。本句意思为"Mary 正处在这么一个阶段，现在她还不能自己洗脸。"

第二部分　完形填空

16. C【解析】本题考查了上下文的衔接。根据第六段倒数第二句可以知道老人有三个儿子，因此，本题的正确选项是 C。

17. D【解析】本题考查了词组辨析。stand by 意为"支持；袖手旁观"；pass by 意为"经过，走过"；go by 意为"经过，顺便拜访"；stop by 意为"路过，逗留"。文章讲的是老人的儿子们只是每周一次到他这稍微停留一会，吃顿饭。因此，本题的正确选项是 D。

18. A【解析】gradually 意为"渐渐地"；clearly 意为"明显地"；fortunately 意为"幸运地"；hurriedly 意为"匆忙地"。后面提到老人越来越虚弱，可见这是一个逐渐变化的过程。因此，本题的正确选项是 A。

19. A【解析】这句话的意思是"他经常担心自己会变成什么样。"

20. D【解析】shelf 意为"书架"；table 意为"桌子"；cupboard 意为"碗柜"；chest 意为

"箱子"。下文提到"The old man took the chest home, ...",可见老人是让木匠朋友帮他做一个大箱子。

21. B【解析】Then the locksmith 在这里是 Then he went to see the locksmith 的省略,可以推测 John 是向锁匠要了一把锁。因此,本题的正确选项是 B。

22. D【解析】根据上下文,这里是指 John 向吹玻璃的人要了他所拥有的所有的玻璃碎片。因此,本题的正确选项是 D。

23. A【解析】这里指的是 John 用碎玻璃把箱子填满直到箱子的顶部。to the top 的意思是"直到最顶端"。

24. C【解析】下文提到"'What's in this chest?' his sons asked, looking under the table."可见 John 是把箱子放到了桌子底下,选项中只有 C 提到了桌子。

25. C【解析】make 意为"制造";keep 意为"保持";save 意为"节省";use 意为"使用"。这里是指保存节省下来的一些东西,下文也提到"It must be full of all the gold he's saved over the years"。

26. A【解析】whisper 意为"耳语,窃窃私语";report 意为"报道";shout 意为"大声喊";point 意为"指出"。根据句意,儿子们是在窃窃私语,谈论 John 的箱子里的物品。

27. D【解析】儿子们以为 John 的箱子里面是金子,所以他们意识到应该看守这些财物,只有选项 D 符合题意。

28. B【解析】take chances 意为"冒险";take turns 意为"轮流,依次";take measures 意为"采取措施,设法";take actions 意为"采取行动,动手"。为了看守财产,儿子们决定轮流和 John 生活在一起。

29. C【解析】on the way 意为"在……途中";by the way 意为"顺便说一下,在途中";that way 意为"那样,那边";in the way 意为"妨碍,挡道"。that way = in that way,在这里指的是通过轮流与 John 共同生活这种方式,儿子们也可以照顾他。

30. A【解析】go on 意为"继续",中间可以有间断;keep on 意为"继续",一直持续下去,没有间断;move on 意为"往前走,前进"。根据常识,儿子们轮流照看父亲不可能没有间断。因此,本题的正确选项是 A。

31. D【解析】根据上下文可知,儿子们是给老人举办了一个很好的葬礼,只有选项 D 符合题意。

32. B【解析】由上文可知,放在床底的是一个大箱子,儿子们以为箱子里放的是金子,这只能是一笔财富。

33. A【解析】service 意为"服务,仪式";celebration 意为"庆祝,庆典";meal 意为"饭";crying 意为"叫喊"。根据上下文,这里指的是葬礼这一仪式结束了。

34. C【解析】mix 意为"混合";paint 意为"绘画";hide 意为"隐藏";grow 意为"生长"。这里指的是最大的儿子把箱子翻了个底朝天想看看是否有值钱的东西藏在碎玻璃里面。

35. B【解析】句意:在底部他找到一个题词写着:尊敬你的父母。read 有"写着,标明"的意思。write"写,写字",更强调写的动作。

第三部分 阅读理解

A

36. C【解析】细节理解题。根据"Jack moved clear across the country in pursuit of his

dreams. There, in the rush of his busy life, Jack had little time to think about the past."可知C项正确。D项错误，因为Jack并没有因为繁忙的生活而完全冲刷了对童年的记忆。B项错误，因为Jack忙得甚至连家人都无法顾及。

37. C【解析】细节理解题。根据Jack母亲的电话内容，很容易选出答案。
38. A【解析】细节理解题。根据"Jack, thanks for your time! Harold Belser."可以判断。
39. D【解析】推理判断题。Jack从Harold Belser对他的感谢中感悟出亲情的重要。这也是文章想表达的主旨。A、B、C文中均未提及。
40. B【解析】归纳概括题。文章以Harold Belser最珍惜的the gold box为线索，表现的是人们最珍惜的应该是人与人之间的感情这个主旨。所以答案选B。

B

41. B【解析】词义题。根据句意不难理解portend是预示的意思。signal也有"显示"的意思；defy意为"不服从，反抗"；suffer from意为"忍受，遭受"；result from意为"由……产生"。
42. D【解析】细节题。题干中的the economy slides等于原文的economic downturns。文中提到经济低迷时期人们倾向推迟婚姻，因为双方不能承担一个家庭或者担心更窘迫的日子。D符合原文意思。
43. C【解析】细节题。第三段最后一句可知答案C正确。
44. A【解析】细节题。第三段第二句提到不能外出工作的妇女会感到被关在笼子里，相当于A项中they feel that they have been robbed of their freedom. 她们感到被剥夺了自由。
45. D【解析】主旨题。用排除法解题。A因果颠倒，排除；B文章从未提及；C以偏概全；只有D，"女性外出工作对婚姻的影响每个个例之间是不一样的"，才准确表达出文章的两种平行的相反观点。

C

46. D【解析】细节题。选项A、B、C均属于内容错误。
47. C【解析】细节题。根据文章第二段"The response to her request for help was so huge that..."一句可知C项正确。根据第三段："In 1993, she was given a Caring Award for her efforts by the Caring Institute."一句可以排除A。根据文章"Poe has also asked the National Park Service to carry out a 'Children's Forest' project in every national park."一句可以排除选项D。
48. B【解析】细节题。根据文章中"Kid's Yards—the creation of backyard wildlife habitats（栖息地）..."一句可知B项正确。其他选项内容与文章不符。
49. D【解析】推理题。题干中关键词为infer, 根据文章最后部分可以得出答案。选项A不属于推断的结果，是文章明确告知的（见文章最后一句话）；选项B无法从文中得出这样的结论；选项C根据文章第二段中"There are now 300,000 members of Kids F. A. C. E. worldwide."一句可以排除。

D

50. C【解析】细节理解题，从第一段第五、六句可知道答案。
51. C【解析】计算判断题，第一段里说一个人起床8个小时后就需要休息，6:30加上8小时应该是下午2:30。

52. B【解析】主旨大意题，全文主要介绍为什么人们在午后容易打瞌睡，建议大家适当的休息一下，有益于身体健康。

E

53. D【解析】文章将美国的售房方式、房屋质量、人均收入与中国对比，说明中国的房价相对于中国的人均收入来说太高了，说明房市存在泡沫。

54. A【解析】前三段说明了中国的房价高，房市存在泡沫，后一段作者列举了政府可以采取的措施来抑制房产泡沫。只有A项点明了这两个方面的意思。

55. B【解析】最后一段作者提到了增加税收、减少对建筑商的贷款和土地征用量、允许人民以多种融资渠道建房，列举了三个方面的措施。

第四部分　写　作

第一节　短文改错

56. √

57. for→of

58. the →a

59. 去掉 of

60. 去掉 a

61. rich→poor

62. Heard→Hearing

63. 去掉 what 或将 what 改为 which /that

64. run→ ran

65. took→take

第二节　书面表达

Dear friends,

　　People often think that water will never be used up. There is plenty of water, such as rain, water from the rivers and wells. In fact, water is rather limited on the earth. With the increase of population and development of industries, water is more needed than before. And a large amount of water has been polluted and wasted every day. Many places in the world are short of water.

　　We should do something about the water shortage. First, we should be aware of the real situation about the water. We have to protect the existing water resources and develop new ones. Laws should be made to protect water. In this way, our cities will not be thirsty for water in the future.

Yours,
Li Ming

Unit 7

Internet

Part One Listening Practice

Section A

1. B	2. B	3. B	4. A	5. A
6. B	7. B	8. B	9. A	10. A
11. A	12. B	13. B	14. B	15. A
16. A	17. B	18. B	19. B	20. A

Section B

Task 1

1) internet   2) be used to   3) chatting with
4) France   5) online shopping

Task 2

6) welcome news   7) signed my employment contract   8) Congratulations to you
9) a salesman   10) a branch manager   11) Congratulate you on your promotion
12) get promoted

Part Two　Detailed Reading

互联网如何改变着我们的生活？

毫无异议地，互联网和其他数字媒体在我们的生活中扮演着一种重要的角色。但是我们是否切实地意识到互联网如何改变我们的生活呢？随着网上信息量的迅速增长，互联网对整个社会都产生了积极的作用。在未来，互联网在我们的生活中扮演的角色将显得越来越重要。

互联网在推动社会进步方面潜力巨大。网上庞大的信息量使得如今一个普通人就能做一项10年前只有专家才能胜任的工作；当今科学家研究员们借助各种网络工具可以完成他们以前料想不到的测试。

众所周知，互联网是一种方便的交流工具。人们在社交网站上，如脸谱网、我的空间等，结识新朋友、联络老朋友。只要使用MSN等瞬时通信软件，不必见面，就能随时与他人聊天，此外还可以发电邮与他人互通消息。交流通信是互联网最重要的功能之一。

很多人在网上看新闻、查信息。在很多新闻网站上，人们可以查询天气预报、交通线路和其他所需信息。人们还可以在网上找到很多所需的信息，如公交车时刻表、商店开放时间等，实在是应有尽有。

网上购物是互联网的另一重大用途。在网上下订单，物品直接能送到家门口，这比去实体店购买要便捷许多，因此，很多人都在亚马逊等网站上买东西。与网上购物一样，如今在网上下载软件也很流行，因为网上有很多软件可以免费下载使用。

互联网的功能强大，信息量庞大。然而，要是信息出错怎么办？像是维基百科，任何人都可以在上面编辑发布，信息出错是极为可能的，为此维基百科要求发布者列出信息出处。但是，要是信息的来源本身是错的，就会导致信息出错了。这种出错的可能性会发生，但有一个简单的解决方法，那就是要求引用相互独立的信息来源，这样可以对照校正。

互联网给我们带来的益处颇多，利远远大于弊。如今互联网的用处是有目共睹的，未来互联网的作用令人期待。互联网改变了我们的生活，其潜力无穷。

Comprehension of the Text

1. B　　　　　2. D　　　　　3. C　　　　　4. B　　　　　5. A

 **Part Three Exercises**

Task 1

1. j   2. d   3. f   4. b   5. g
6. c   7. e   8. i   9. h   10. a

Task 2

1. convenient   2. publishing   3. digit   4. downloaded   5. play a role
6. advantage   7. corresponding with 8. cited   9. alternates   10. potential

Task 3

1. Have you been <u>corresponding with</u> your high school classmates?
2. The Internet is <u>playing an important role</u> in our study and lives.
3. Misunderstanding is caused by lack of <u>communication</u>.
4. Online shopping is becoming more and more <u>popular</u> among people, esp. young people.
5. Generally speaking, the <u>advantages</u> of the Internet are greater than the <u>disadvantages</u>.

Task 4   Writing

Dec. 19th

Dear Mr. David,

    Christmas is around the corner. Our department is going to hold an English Evening Party at Student's Center from 7:00 to 9:00 this Friday (Dec. 24th). Would you and Mrs. Stanley come and enjoy the evening with us? We are looking forward to your arrival.

Yours sincerely,
Xiao Yu

Unit 7

Part Four Supplementary Reading

译 文

戒 除 网 瘾

对于网瘾这件事，有人嗤之以鼻，也有人如临大敌。即使不像其他类的上瘾有损健康，但是它妨碍了人们的工作和生活，确实成了一个令人头疼的问题。如果你染上了网瘾，要果断地戒除它，不要好似掉进蜘蛛网苦苦挣扎的苍蝇一般。

第一步：要正视问题。想一想你在完全没有必要的时候，是不是总要查看邮箱，反复地登录同一家网站？你每天上网浏览网页是否占用了太长的时间？

第二步：找出原由。上网比喝酒要便宜方便，又不像吸毒是非法行为。然而上网与醉酒吸毒一样是在逃避问题。认识到这些以后，就会发现上网成瘾是一件严重的事情，而不是被人所嘲笑那样不是什么"真正的"上瘾。

第三步：少上网。当然，说比做要容易得多。虽然无法做到不看电邮、不登录网站，但是你可以减少查看电邮的次数。这种方法也适用于聊天室、游戏、在线赌博、交友网以及其他占据你时间的网站。给自己规定每天用电脑的最长时间。

第四步：不要待在办公室或是家里，而是出去散步、就餐，尽量远离电脑。休息一段时间有助于头脑清醒。要是电脑能接收无线信号，出去时一定不要带上电脑。

第五步：做些不用上网的活动填补空闲，比如尝试新爱好、读读书、与朋友一起玩、健身等。

下面是一些建议与提醒。

与其他上瘾一样，得知有人与自己同病相怜会令人心有戚戚然。因此可以去互助小组与他人一起戒除网瘾。

以往通过发电邮的形式与人来往，现在可以改成打电话，见面也行。

像其他上瘾一样，最重要的是要找到你到底在逃避什么，网瘾只不过是症状，要追根溯源。

要是上述这些都不起作用的话，一定要去看专业的心理医生。对网瘾若是不闻不顾，最后极可能和酗酒吸毒一样酿成悲剧。

Comprehension of the Text

1. Internet addiction will be a problem if it gets in the way of your work or social life.
2. You can reduce frequency of checking email, and set the maximum amount you use the

computer a day.

3. If the tips mentioned above failed, you should seek professional counseling.

自我测试题

第一部分　单项填空

从［A］、［B］、［C］、［D］四个选项中，选出可以填入空白处的最佳选项，并在答题卡上将该项涂黑。

> **Example:**
> It is generally considered unwise to give a child _____ he or she wants.
> ［A］however　　　［B］whatever　　　［C］whichever　　　［D］whenever
> **Answer:** ［A］ [■] ［C］［D］

1. —_____
   —Fine, I've got used to the life there and I've made some friends.
   ［A］How are you?　　　　　　　　　［B］How are you doing?
   ［C］Are you getting on well?　　　　［D］How do you do?
2. There was _____ time _____ I hated to go to school.
   ［A］a; that　　　［B］a; when　　　［C］the; that　　　［D］the; when
3. —Which share is meant for me? —You can take _____ half. They are exactly the same.
   ［A］this　　　［B］any　　　［C］each　　　［D］neither
4. He has got himself into a dangerous situation _____ he is likely to lose control over the plan.
   ［A］when　　　［B］which　　　［C］where　　　［D］why
5. If you want to sell your product, you must _____ it.
   ［A］advertise　　　［B］advertise for　　　［C］advertise on　　　［D］advertise to
6. How many of us _____ a meeting that is not important to us would be interested in the discussion?
   ［A］attended　　　［B］attending　　　［C］to attend　　　［D］have attended
7. Why does teaching as a career _____ many people?
   ［A］apply for　　　［B］attract to　　　［C］appeal to　　　［D］agree with
8. He is _____ a good teacher. He is also his students' good friend.
   ［A］no more than　　　［B］not more than　　　［C］no less than　　　［D］more than
9. The husband rushed to the hospital _____ he heard that his wife was injured.
   ［A］at the moment　　　［B］for the moment　　　［C］in a moment　　　［D］the moment
10. The soldier was _____ of running away when the enemy attached.

  [A] scolded   [B] charged   [C] accused   [D] punished

11. It _____ how long the shock that explosions hit London transport system will stay in people's hearts.

  [A] abandons   [B] considers   [C] matters   [D] minds

12. The police got to _____ was once an old school _____ the peasants used as a store.

  [A] what; that   [B] where; which   [C] where; that   [D] which; where

13. —Are there any English story-books for us students in the library?

  —There are only a few, _____.

  [A] if any   [B] if some   [C] if many   [D] if much

14. —Why not play the music we listened to yesterday?

  —Because it _____ old times.

  [A] call on   [B] calls for   [C] calls in   [D] calls up

15. _____ your budget, keep a careful record of each dollars you spend every day.

  [A] Follow   [B] To follow   [C] Following   [D] Followed

第二部分　完形填空

  阅读下面短文，从短文后所给的四个选项（[A]、[B]、[C]、[D]）中选出能填入相应空白处的最佳选项，并在答题卡上将该项涂黑。

  As she walked round the large shop, Edith realized how difficult it was to choose a suitable Christmas __16__ for her father.

  She __17__ that he were as easy to please as her mother, who was __18__ satisfied with perfume（香水）. __19__, shopping at this time of the year was a most __20__ job. People __21__ on your feet, pushed you with their shoulders and almost __22__ you over in their hurry in order to __23__ something cheap ahead of you.

  Partly to have a rest, Edith paused in front of a counter, where some beautiful ties were on __24__. "They are __25__ silk." the shop assistant told her with a smile trying to __26__ her to buy one. But Edith knew from past __27__ that her choice of ties hardly ever pleased her father.

  She moved on slowly and then, quite by chance, __28__ where a small crowd of men had gathered round a counter. She found some fine pipes on sale and the __29__ were very beautiful. Edith did not hesitate for long, although her father __30__ smoked a pipe once in a while, she believed this was __31__ to please him.

  When she got home, with her small but __32__ present hidden in her handbag, it was time for supper and her parents were already __33__ table. Her mother was in great __34__. "Your father has at last decided to stop smoking." she told her daughter happily. Edith was so __35__ that she could not say a single word.

16. [A] suit   [B] card   [C] thing   [D] gift

17. [A] believed   [B] wished   [C] hoped   [D] supposed

18. [A] never   [B] seldom   [C] always   [D] scarcely

19. [A]	Therefore	[B]	Fortunately	[C]	Besides	[D]	Finally
20. [A]	unhappy	[B]	careful	[C]	exciting	[D]	tiring
21. [A]	walked	[B]	stepped	[C]	lifted	[D]	stood
22. [A]	turned	[B]	hit	[C]	brought	[D]	knocked
23. [A]	watch	[B]	find	[C]	grasp	[D]	sell
24. [A]	time	[B]	show	[C]	board	[D]	duty
25. [A]	real	[B]	cheap	[C]	poor	[D]	exact
26. [A]	hope	[B]	ask	[C]	force	[D]	persuade
27. [A]	experience	[B]	things	[C]	books	[D]	school
28. [A]	stopped	[B]	saw	[C]	asked	[D]	found
29. [A]	money	[B]	cigarette	[C]	shapes	[D]	shop
30. [A]	always	[B]	nearly	[C]	only	[D]	never
31. [A]	hardly	[B]	impossibly	[C]	possibly	[D]	certainly
32. [A]	cheap	[B]	well-chosen	[C]	expensive	[D]	ready-made
33. [A]	on	[B]	by	[C]	beside	[D]	at
34. [A]	excitement	[B]	anger	[C]	sadness	[D]	disappointment
35. [A]	glad	[B]	happy	[C]	surprised	[D]	excited

第三部分 阅读理解

阅读下列短文，从每题所给的四个选项（[A]、[B]、[C]、[D]）中选出最佳选项，并在答题卡上将该项涂黑。

A

The United States is one of the few countries in the world that has an official day on which fathers are honored by their children. On the third Sunday in June, fathers all across or otherwise made to feel special.

However, the idea for creating a day for children to honor their fathers began in Spokane, Washington. A woman by the name of Sonora Smart Dodd thought of the idea for father's day while listening to a mother's day sermon in 1909. Having been raised by her father, Henry Jackson Smart, after her mother died, Sonora wanted her father to know how special he was to her. It was her father that made all the parental sacrifices and was, in the eyes of his daughter, a selfless and loving man. Sonora's father was born in June, so she chose to hold the first father's day celebration in Spokane, Washington on the 19th of June, 1910.

In 1924 President Calvin Coolidge declared the third Sunday in June as father's day. Roses are the father's day flowers, red to be worn for a living father and white if the father has died.

When children can't visit their fathers or take them out to dinner, they send a greeting card. Traditionally, fathers prefer greeting cards that are not too sentimental. Most greeting cards are too special so fathers laugh when they open them. Some give heartfelt thanks for being there whenever the child needed dad.

36. The United States is special in father's day because _____ .

 [A] many people celebrate the day   [B] only America celebrates the day

 [C] America makes it an official day   [D] all men are honored in America

37. At first, father's day was fixed on June 19th because _____ .

 [A] Sonora honored her father's birthday

 [B] Sonora's birthday was June 19

 [C] it was decided by the president at that time

 [D] her mother died on June 19

38. How many years has passed before father's day became an official day since the father's day was celebrated?

 [A] 4.   [B] 10.   [C] 14.   [D] 24.

39. According to the passage, on father's day, _____ .

 [A] people will wear the same flowers to honor their fathers

 [B] only daughters wear red flowers to honors their fathers

 [C] children must go home to honor their fathers

 [D] fathers are often honored in different ways

40. According to the passage, we can infer that Henry Jackson Smart _____ .

 [A] was very kind to anyone   [B] did a lot for his daughter

 [C] was the first father honored in 1924   [D] always helps others by giving money

B

Put an ice cube from your fridge into a glass of water. You have a piece of string (线) 10 centimeters long. The problem is to take out that piece of ice with the help of the string. But you must not touch the ice with your fingers.

You may ask your friends to try to do that when you are having dinner together. There is a saltcellar on the table. You must use salt when you carry out this experiment.

First you put the string across the piece of ice. Then put some salt on the ice. Salt makes ice melt. The ice round the string will begin to melt. But when it melts, it will lose heat. The cold ice cube will make the salt water freeze again.

After a minute or two you may raise the piece of string and with it you will raise your piece of ice!

This experiment can be very useful to you. If, for example, there is ice near the door of your house, you must use very much salt to melt all the ice. If you don't put enough salt, the water will freeze again.

41. We must use _____ when we carry out this experiment.

 [A] fridge   [B] some food   [C] a table   [D] some salt

42. How long will it take to carry out this experiment?

 [A] More than three minutes.   [B] Five minutes or so.

[C] Only one minute or two. [D] About ten minutes.

43. What is the task of this experiment?

   [A] Put the ice cube into the glass of water with the help of the string.

   [B] Take out the ice cube in the glass of water with the help of the string.

   [C] Take out the ice cube in the glass of water with your fingers.

   [D] Put some salt on the ice cube and then put the string across it.

44. How many things at least are used in this experiment?

   [A] Three.　　　　[B] Four.　　　　[C] Six.　　　　[D] Seven.

45. We can learn something about _____ from the passage.

   [A] physics　　　[B] biology　　　[C] chemistry　　　[D] maths

C

The income gap between China's rural and urban residents has continued to widen during the past few years in spite of rapidly rising rural incomes, Agricultural Minister Sun Zhengcai said here on Wednesday.

The income ratio between urban and rural residents was 3.28:1 in 2006, against 3.23:1 in 2003, said Sun in his report on the promotion of building a new countryside in 2007. Sun also said the net income of rural residents in different regions also varied widely.

The income gap is only one of several problems in rural areas, according to Sun's report. While listing the achievements in rural areas in recent years, Sun believed that rural development still fall behind urban development.

"We have bigger pressure to ensure the supply of major agricultural products such as grain," he said. "China's urbanization (都市化) has been speeded up and more rural residents have gone to urban areas." he said.

"In this case, more agricultural producers become farm produce consumers, which created more pressure for supply." he said.

Another problem facing China's agricultural development is inadequate application of science and technology.

"Only 30 percent of scientific and technological achievements have been applied to agricultural production, which is 40 percentage points lower than developed countries." he said.

Despite increased government spending in rural areas, the infrastructure (基础设施) is still poor and easily hit by disasters.

According to Sun, the government spent 431.8 billion Yuan ($59.15 billion) on agriculture, rural areas and farmers this year, an increase of 80.1 billion Yuan over the previous year.

China set aside 11.38 billion Yuan to promote a new rural cooperative medical care system and 27.98 billion Yuan to support the new compulsory education mechanism in rural area to ensure that all citizens shared the fruits of China's reform and opening-up, Sun said.

46. Which of the following is TRUE according to the text?

   [A] Because of the rapidly rising rural incomes, the income gap between China's rural and

urban residents will disappear this year.
- [B] The net income of rural residents in different regions is the same.
- [C] The government has taken measures to develop the economy in the rural areas.
- [D] Because of the rapidly rising rural incomes, the supply of major agricultural products is enough.

47. Can you infer the meaning of the underlined words in paragraph 6?
    - [A] Be made full use of.
    - [B] Be made little use of.
    - [C] Be not made full use of.
    - [D] Be made good use of.

48. How much is spent on agriculture, rural areas and farmers the previous year?
    - [A] 431.8 billion Yuan.
    - [B] 511.9 billion Yuan.
    - [C] 351.7 billion Yuan.
    - [D] 80.1 billion Yuan.

49. Which is NOT the problem in rural areas?
    - [A] The income gap.
    - [B] The inadequate application of science and technology.
    - [C] The supply of major agricultural products.
    - [D] China's urbanization.

D

Paracutin was born in Mexico in February, 1943. At the end of one week Paracutin was 500 feet high, and it is now over 9,000 feet high. Today Paracutin is asleep.

What is Paracutin? It was the first volcano (火山) in the world which was seen from its birth right up to the present day. On February 20, 1943, a peasant and his wife set out to work in their corn fields from the Mexican village of Paracutin. They were surprised to find the earth warm under their feet. Suddenly they heard noises deep in the earth and a small hole appeared in their field. In the afternoon there was a sudden loud noise and stones were thrown high in the air. The peasants ran from the field and turned to watch. They saw the birth of a volcano.

Large quantities of stone and lava (岩浆) broke out and a little hill began to form. By evening this hill was 100 feet high and hot ashes (灰烬) were falling on the village. At night the strong light of the hot lava lit up the countryside. The trees near the village were killed and the villagers had to leave their houses. When the village was destroyed, its name was given to the volcano. The news quickly reached Mexico City, far to the east. Many people came to watch the scene. The volcano grew and grew for ten years and hundreds of square miles of forest were destroyed. Then Paracutin went to sleep.

50. What was destroyed in the growing up of the volcano?
    - [A] The little hill of stone.
    - [B] The villagers living close by.
    - [C] The forests and fields round Paracutin.
    - [D] The Mexican peasant and his wife.

51. In this passage the writer is trying to _____.
    - [A] tell us an interesting happening
    - [B] explain a scientific theory
    - [C] make us believe something
    - [D] make up an interesting story

52. What can we learn about volcanoes from this passage?

[A] New volcanoes may appear in places where people do not expect them to be.

[B] Volcanoes are always growing.

[C] Volcanoes are active from time to time.

[D] New volcanoes are active for only ten years.

E

Vienna—In spite of Iraq's decision to stop oil deliveries, the 11-nation Organization of Petroleum Exporting Countries (OPEC) will not increase production to make up the shortfall, ministers decided Tuesday in Vienna.

The 11 oil ministers decided to meet again on July 3 to discuss the effects of the Iraq temporary stop. The organization's president, Charkid Kheria of Algeria, said after the meeting that stocks were high and prices were stable, so quota increases were not necessary.

The E. U. Commission has expressed concern about Iraq's output stop. A speaker said OPEC had to take all possible measures to keep or lower the oil price.

Saudi Arabia's Oil Minister Ali Al-Nuaimi had earlier said there would not be any shortfall of oil in the market. The organization had already taken steps to fill the gap, he said. OPEC Secretary General Ali Rodriguez added that the period of Iraq's output stop was not known, so other exporters were not going to lift quotas yet. If the market was destabilized (使……动摇), a suitable response could be made.

Iraq on Monday stopped shipments of crude oil to protest against the U. N. Security Council's decision to extend the oil-for-food program by only a month, instead of the normal six-month renewal. Just before the Vienna meeting, oil prices had gone up, with a barrel of OPEC crude oil selling for 27.05 dollars, up from 26.81 dollars last Friday. North Sea oil was at 29.26 dollars Monday evening.

OPEC wants the oil price to stay within a margin of 22 to 28 dollars and achieved that with cuts in January and March that reduced 2.5 million barrels per day off quotas (配额).

53. Iraq made the decision to stop oil deliveries because _____.

[A] oil price is too low in international market

[B] the U. N. Secretary Council has decided to shorten the time of extension of the oil-for-food program

[C] many oil wells were destroyed during the war in the late 1980s

[D] it couldn't get enough money to develop its economy

54. The 11 oil ministers decided to meet on July 3 so that _____.

[A] they can persuade Iraq to continue oil production

[B] they can have a talk with the U. N. Security Council

[C] they can have a discussion about the effects of Iraq's temporary output stop

[D] they can make up their minds to increase oil production

55. The main idea of the passage is _____.

［A］ the oil prices in the world were stable though Iraq has stopped oil deliveries

［B］ OPEC has controlled the oil price to stay within a margin of 22 to 28 dollars

［C］ OPEC will not increase oil production to make up the shortfall that caused by Iraq

［D］ oil is connected with people's daily life

第四部分　写　　作

第一节　短文改错

此题要求改正所给短文中的错误。对标有题号的每一行做出判断：如无错误，在该行右边横线上画一个勾（√）；如有错误（每行只有一个错误），则按下列情况改正：

此行多一个词：把多余的词用斜线（\）划掉，在该行右边横线上写出该词，并也用斜线划掉。

此行缺一个词：在缺词处加一个漏字符号（∧），在该行右边横线上写出该加的词。

此行错一个词：在错的词下画一横线，在该行右边横线上写出改正后的词。

注意：原行没有错的不要改。

After supper Li Hua came and asked for me	56. _____
to go and see a film with him. In our way to	57. _____
the cinema we saw a little girl sit by the	58. _____
roadside cry. We bought her a cake to stop	59. _____
her crying. But when we asked where she	60. _____
had lived she said she didn't know. So we took	61. _____
her to the police station and asked police to take care of her.	62. _____
After this we went to the cinema. But when we	63. _____
got there the movie was near at its end.	64. _____
We have missed the movie, but we did a good deed.	65. _____

第二节　书面表达

假定你是李明。英国著名语言学家 Mr. Louis Alexander 应邀来京讲学，并到你校参观，和一些学生座谈。现由你主持座谈会，代表你校学生用英语致欢迎词。

要点如下：

1. 对来访客人表示热烈欢迎；

2. 介绍 Mr. Louis Alexander 及其著作，包括大家熟知的《新概念英语》（New Concept English）、《跟我学》（Follow Me）等；

3. 介绍 Mr. Louis Alexander 来京目的；

4. 请 Mr. Alexander 作指导，提建议；

5. 请大家就英语学习方面的问题向他提问。

参考词汇如下：

语言学家：linguist

讲学：give a lecture

注意：词数 100 个左右。

参考答案及解析

第一部分 单项填空

1. B【解析】A 询问身体状况，B 询问工作进展或生活情况如何，从答句"已适应那儿的生活"可知 B 正确。C 是一般疑问句。

2. B【解析】a time 表示"曾经，一度"，when 引导的定语从句修饰 a time。
There was a time when this song was very popular.
There was a time when women were not admitted to universities.

3. B【解析】从 half 可知是两半，意思是"你可以拿任何一半"，还可用 either。

4. C【解析】situation，case，point 等词后常用 where 引导定语从句；occasion 后常用 when 引导定语从句。

5. A【解析】advertise sth. "为……登广告，登广告宣传……"；advertise for sth. (sb.) "登广告征求或寻找某物或某人"，比较：advertise jobs "登广告招人"；advertise for jobs "登广告求职"。

6. B【解析】attending a meeting that is not important to us 作定语。

7. C【解析】apply for "申请"，attract "吸引"，attract sb./sth. to "把……吸引到……"，appeal to "对……有诱惑力"。

8. D【解析】no more than = only；not more than "不超过"；no less than = as much as；more than = not only。

9. D【解析】名词引导时间状语从句，the moment = the minute/the instant = immediately/directly (adv.) = as soon as (conj.)。

10. C【解析】be accused of = be charged with "被指控……"；be scolded/punished for…"因……而被责骂/惩罚"。

11. C【解析】考查动词辨析。句意为：袭击伦敦交通系统所带来的震惊在人们的内心会持续多长时间那是最要紧的。it 是形式主语，matter "要紧；至关重要"。

12. A【解析】what 等于 the place，that 后为 that 引导的定语从句。

13. A【解析】if any 是 if there are any books 的省略句，意思是说"如果有书的话，也只有几本"。

14. D【解析】本题考查动词短语，call up 意为"使人回想起"。call on 意为"拜访某人；号召某人做什么"；call for 意为"要求"；call in 意为"请进来"。

15. B【解析】本题考查非谓语动词。句子意思是："为了和开支预算相符合"，表示目的，要用动词不定式。

第二部分 完形填空

16. D【解析】由下文可知，Edith 在为父亲选择一件圣诞节礼物。

17. B【解析】由宾语从句中的谓语动词 were 可知，这是虚拟语气，主句的谓语动词应该是 wish。

18. C【解析】根据"he were as easy to please as her mother"，可知应该填 always。

Unit 7

19. C【解析】Besides "除此以外"。
20. A【解析】本题考查形容词词义辨析 unhappy "不乐意的"。
21. B【解析】本题考查动词词义辨析，由上文可知，应选择 stepped。
22. D【解析】本题考查动词词义辨析，由句意可知，应选择 knocked。
23. B【解析】给父亲选择一件合适的礼物很难，而且，时值圣诞节购物高峰，买东西不是一件令人愉快的事情，人们踩到你的脚上，用肩膀挤着你，为了能在你的前面买到便宜货，几乎会把你撞倒。
24. B【解析】be on show 是固定词组，意为 "陈列着"。
25. A【解析】领带是真丝的。
26. D【解析】persuade "劝说；说服"。
27. A【解析】售货员试图说服 Edith 买一条领带，但从过去的经验中她知道她选择的领带很难使父亲满意。
28. A【解析】Edith 在一些男人聚集的柜台前停下来。
29. C【解析】烟斗的形状很好看。
30. C【解析】only "仅仅"。
31. D【解析】尽管父亲只是偶尔使用烟斗吸烟，但她认为这个烟斗肯定会使父亲满意。
32. B【解析】从上文可知，这份小礼物是精心挑选的。
33. D【解析】be at table 是固定词组，表 "坐在桌子旁"。
34. A【解析】由 "she told her daughter happily" 可知，因为父亲决定戒烟，母亲很高兴。
35. C【解析】Edith 对父亲戒烟感到惊讶，因为她给父亲买的礼物又不合适了。

第三部分　阅读理解

A

36. C【解析】从文章的第一段第一句可知。
37. A【解析】从文章的第二段第五句可知。
38. C【解析】从第二段的最后一句和第三段的第一句可知。
39. D【解析】从文章的最后两段可知。
40. B【解析】文章的第二段提到，她的父亲无私、仁慈，她母亲死后，是父亲把她养大的，因此可知她的父亲一定对她做了很多。

B

41. D【解析】我们进行实验时必须用什么？文章第二段最后一句说当进行实验时你必须用 salt（盐）。由此可知答案是 D。
42. C【解析】文章第四段提到 "After a minute or two...（一两分钟后你可以提起细绳⋯⋯）"，由此可知进行这个实验仅需一两分钟时间。
43. B【解析】题目问这个实验的任务是什么呢？由文章第一段第三句 "The problem is to take out that piece of ice with the help of the string（问题是如何用细绳将冰块拿出）"，可知答案为 B。
44. B【解析】题目问实验中至少用了几样东西？从全文可知道至少用了 string, salt, a glass of water, ice cube 这 4 种东西。

45. C【解析】题目问通过这段文字我们了解了一些什么知识？实验用 salt 把 ice 融化，这应属于化学变化。

C

46. C【解析】文章最后一段提到了政府对农村的投入，可知政府采取了措施来发展乡村经济。

47. C【解析】由接下来提到应用的比率及这个比率与发达国家的比较，可知应用得并不充分，但也不是只有一点儿。

48. C【解析】今年是431.8，比去年增长了80.1，那么去年应当是这两个数的差，即351.7。

49. D【解析】文中提到中国的城市化引起了农村人口的流动，这是引起农村问题的原因，不是问题本身。

D

50. C【解析】。细节题。根据第三段倒数第二句"The volcano grew and grew for ten years and hundreds of square miles of forest were destroyed"可知答案选 C。

51. A【解析】判断题。此题可用排除法做，选项 B、C、D 显然与原文不符，故选 A。

52. A【解析】判断题。根据文章内容和一般常识可以排除选项 B、C 和 D，而且从文章中我们可以了解到那个村庄没有人知道会有火山爆发，所以答案选 A。

E

53. ［B］由文章倒数第二段第一句可知。
54. ［C］文章第二段第一句说明。
55. ［C］文章开头就点明了 OPEC 对伊拉克暂停供油的态度，下文又进行了分析。

第四部分　写　　作

第一节　短文改错

56. 去掉 for
57. In→On
58. sit→sitting/seated
59. cry→crying
60. √
61. 去掉 had
62. （第二个）police 前加 the
63. this→that
64. near→nearly
65. 去掉 have

第二节　书面表达

Dear schoolmates,

　　I am Li Ming. First of all, let's give our warmest welcome to our honorable guest—Mr. Louis Alexander. Mr. Louis Alexander is a world-famous English linguist. He's written lots of works, including *New Concept English*, *Follow Me* and so on. All these are well known to us all. Mr. Alexander is invited to Beijing to give lectures and today he's going to have a talk with us to get a further understanding of English study in middle schools in China. If you have any questions on English, you are free to ask him for help. Now let's invite Mr. Alexander to give us a talk and give us advice on English study.

That's all. Thank you!

Unit 8

Entertainment

Part One   Listening Practice

Section A

1. A 2. D 3. A 4. C 5. A

Section B

6. B 7. D 8. D 9. D 10. C

Section C

11) guests
14) serving
12) all kinds of
15) improving
13) business center

Section D

1) last night
4) can't agree more
2) What a pity
5) as if
3) the best films

Unit 8

Part Two   Detailed Reading

译 文

《花生漫画》之父——查尔斯·舒兹

2000年2月,《花生漫画》之父查尔斯·舒兹逝世,享年77岁,全世界成千上万的《花生》迷们闻讯悲痛不已。这位漫画大师生前创造了查理·布朗和其爱犬史努比的经典形象,月前因健康状况不佳退休。

查尔斯·舒兹于1950年开始创作《花生》系列漫画,这套漫画最早发表在美国的7家报纸上,50年来,《花生》给无数的人们带来了欢乐。最初之时,漫画就以孩子和小动物为主题,历久不变。人们爱上了故事的主角们,因为在角色身上见到了自己的影子,他们有优缺点,也有喜怒哀乐。比如,故事的主角查理缺乏自信,遇事易紧张,经常把事情搞得一团糟,连放风筝也不会,棒球赛总是输,足球也踢不好,但是他凡事总是全力以赴,不轻言放弃。

查理养了一条狗,名叫史努比,史努比大概比查理还要受读者们的爱戴。史努比是个有趣的角色,它梦想着成为一位作家,写出一部巨著,可它总是一遍遍地写"天黑了,暴风雨来了",之后便没了下文。《花生》中还有其他令人难忘的角色。露茜不信任任何人;史洛德喜欢弹玩具钢琴,每年都要纪念贝多芬的诞辰;莱纳斯没有安全感,总是毛毯不离身;派伯敏特·佩蒂非常有运动天赋,对查理颇有好感。

舒兹说在这些角色身上也有他自己的影子,比如查理老是遭遇失败、史努比的幽默、露茜有时会脾气失控、莱纳斯没有安全感,这些在他自己身上或多或少都有。漫画里有些故事的灵感也取自他的一些亲身经历。

几十年来,舒兹独立创作了大概18 000本漫画,作为漫画家,这实在是件了不起的事。他还为根据《花生》改编的电视或电影作品写了剧本,大约有50多部动画片是由《花生》改编的,《花生》也形成了一个产业,很多玩具、游戏、衣服和贺卡是由《花生》衍生出来的。

2002年,查尔斯·舒兹纪念馆在加州圣罗莎落成,在那里人们可以瞻仰《花生》的手稿,深入了解这位大师的生活与创作。纪念馆里有一间房间,再现了舒兹画画时书房的样子,另一些房间里陈列着他的遗物和所获的奖项。他的遗孀希望人们在纪念馆里不仅能够看到他的作品,更能了解他的生活。同时,纪念馆里还展示了由其他画家创作的向《花生》致敬的一些作品。

Comprehension of the Text

1. C   2. D   3. C   4. B   5. D

Part Three Exercises

Task 1

1. d   2. g   3. f   4. i   5. h
6. j   7. b   8. c   9. e   10. a

Task 2

1. celebrate   2. popular   3. memorable   4. demonstrate   5. based on
6. retired   7. character   8. humor   9. composer   10. lack

Task 3

1. She mistrusted her ability to drive.
2. Is that ladder secure?
3. They celebrated his success by opening a bottle of wine.
4. Has anything unusual happened?
5. Children should honour their parents.

Task 4

Feb. 15, 2010

Dear Mr. & Mrs. Frank,

    Many thanks for your warm invitation to the celebration party of the 10th anniversary of your marriage. The warmth and romance at the party impressed me so much that I've got an unforgettable evening. I admire your couple so much. Best wishes to you both for a long and happy life!

    I really appreciate your hospitality.

Yours sincerely

Zhang Lei

Unit 8

Part Four　Supplementary Reading

译　文

芭比娃娃

　　20世纪50年代初期，汉德勒就发现女儿芭芭拉和小伙伴们不仅喜欢玩婴儿娃娃，也喜欢或更偏爱玩大人娃娃。她意识到家长灌输女孩形象意识和学习照顾孩子一样要紧。

　　那时大人玩偶有的是纸糊的，有的是厚纸板做的，汉德勒便想为女儿和她的小伙伴制造一种立体的大人娃娃。她把这个主意告诉了美泰公司的主管们，这家公司是她和丈夫埃利奥特几年前在自家车库成立的。可是所有的主管（都是男士）都否决了这个想法，因为成本太高，市场潜力也不大。

　　不久后，汉德勒到欧洲旅行时，带回一款叫莉莉的娃娃，这种娃娃的原型是德国一部漫画作品的人物。汉德勒花时间设计了另一款与莉莉相似的娃娃，芭比娃娃（以汉德勒女儿的名字命名）就这样诞生了，这款娃娃以"邻家女孩"的形象示人。

　　公司终于答应支持汉德勒的工作。而芭比娃娃上市第一年就卖出351 000个，创造了公司的销售记录。现在，芭比娃娃每年有超过100万的销售量，是玩具市场中畅销最久的玩具。

　　后来，有其他亲戚朋友陆续加入到芭比娃娃系列里，包括Ken（1961年，以汉德勒的儿子的名字命名）、Midge（1963年）、Skipper（1956年）还有黑人娃娃克里斯蒂（1968年）。近些年间，1995年芭比有了一个小妹妹——小婴儿凯利，两年后又认识了一位坐轮椅的残疾好友——微笑的贝基。

　　今日，芭比不仅仅只是玩具。孩子们使用芭比公司的软件可以在电脑上发挥想象力和创造力，自己设计制作娃娃。芭比公司还开发了很多与芭比配套的玩具产品，有芭比书、衣服、食物、家具和家用电子产品，这些产品令孩子们兴奋不已。

　　玩芭比娃娃可以提升女孩子的自我形象，开发她们的潜能，随着芭比自己做了医生、消防员、宇航员、企业家、警察和运动员等，这种说法越发真实，否决了女孩玩芭比娃娃无益的说法。芭比娃娃确实是史上最畅销的玩具娃娃。

Comprehension of the Text

1. They thought it was too expensive to produce the doll and also there would be little potential for wide market appeal.
2. Handler designed the Barbie doll which is similar to a "Lilli" doll and it is a small model of the "girl next door."
3. It can improve girls' self-image and expand their sense of their potential.

自我测试题

第一部分 单项填空

从 [A]、[B]、[C]、[D] 四个选项中，选出可以填入空白处的最佳选项，并在答题卡上将该项涂黑。

> **Example:**
> It is generally considered unwise to give a child _____ he or she wants.
>   [A] however   [B] whatever   [C] whichever   [D] whenever
> **Answer:** [A] [■] [C] [D]

1. Sit on the edge of _____ bed _____ minute before putting your feet on the floor.
    [A] /; a   [B] /; the   [C] the; the   [D] the; a
2. —Is that the small company you often refer to?
    —Right, just the one _____ you know I used to work for years.
    [A] that   [B] which   [C] as   [D] where
3. His grandfather was among the first to settle in _____ is now a famous holiday center.
    [A] what   [B] which   [C] where   [D] that
4. David arrived at the meeting _____ at ten o'clock, as it was scheduled, not a minute early or late.
    [A] flexibly   [B] temporarily   [C] approximately   [D] punctually
5. Get involved in sports or other activities you enjoy _____ you can meet people who like what you like.
    [A] what   [B] when   [C] that   [D] where
6. Reality is not the way you wish things to be, nor the way they appear to be, _____ the way they actually are.
    [A] as   [B] or   [C] but   [D] and
7. To save class time, our teacher has _____ students do half of the exercises in class and complete the other half for homework.
    [A] us   [B] we   [C] our   [D] ours
8. We live day by day, but in the great things, the time of days and weeks _____ so small that a day is unimportant.
    [A] is   [B] are   [C] has been   [D] have been
9. —I'm sorry to keep you waiting. I'll make short work of this.
    — _____. I'm not in a hurry.

[A] Take it easy [B] Take your time
[C] Not at all [D] Do as you like

10. Facts prove that the world's economic development is not a win-lose game but one in which all _____ be winners.
   [A] can [B] shall [C] must [D] would

11. —Were all the toys for the children carried to their kindergarten?
    —No, _____ only some of them.
   [A] it was [B] they were [C] there were [D] there was

12. —Why are they taking all the equipment away?
    —The job _____, they are packing up to leave.
   [A] done [B] being done [C] was done [D] having done

13. With that trust _____ to serve all Americans and I will do my best to fulfill that duty every day as your President.
   [A] coming a duty [B] which comes a duty
   [C] comes a duty [D] a duty came

14. I'll _____ his reputation among the business in the community, and then make a decision whether or not to approve a loan.
   [A] take care of [B] take into account [C] take notice of [D] put up with

15. —How have you been doing recently?
    —_____. Nothing really goes wrong.
   [A] Good luck [B] I'll keep my fingers crossed
   [C] Can't complain [D] So long

第二部分 完形填空

阅读下面短文，从短文后所给的四个选项（[A]、[B]、[C]、[D]）中选出能填入相应空白处的最佳选项，并在答题卡上将该项涂黑。

I was 15 when I walked into McCarley's Bookstore in Ashland. As I was looking at   16   on the shelves, the man behind the counter,   17 , asked if I'd like   18 . I needed to start   19   for college, so I said yes. I   20   after school and during summers for the lowest wages and the job helped pay for my freshman year of college. I would work many other jobs; I made coffee in the Students Union during college; I was a hotel maid and even made maps for the U. S. Forest Service. But selling books was one of the most   21 . One day a woman asked me for books on cancer. She seemed fearful. I showed her almost   22   we had at that time   23   and found other books we could order. She left the store less   24 . I've always remembered the   25   I felt in having helped her.

Years later, as a   26   in Los Angeles, I heard about an immigrant child who was born with his fingers connected, weblike. His family could not   27   a corrective operation, and the boy lived in   28 , hiding his hand in his pocket.

I 29 my boss to let me do the story. After my story was broadcast, a doctor and a nurse called, offering to perform the 30 for free.

I visited the boy in the recovery room soon after the operation. The first thing he did was to hold up his 31 hand and say, "Thank you." I felt a sense of 32 .

In the past, while I was 33 , I always sense I was working for the customers, not the store. Today it's the same. NBC News pays my salary, 34 I feel as if I work for the 35 , helping them make sense of the world.

16. [A] maps [B] titles [C] articles [D] reports
17. [A] the reader [B] the college student [C] the shop owner [D] the customer
18. [A] a book [B] a job [C] some tea [D] any help
19. [A] planning [B] saving [C] preparing [D] studying
20. [A] read [B] studied [C] cooked [D] worked
21. [A] boring [B] surprising [C] satisfying [D] disappointing
22. [A] anything [B] something [C] nothing [D] everything
23. [A] in need [B] in all [C] in order [D] in store
24. [A] worried [B] satisfied [C] excited [D] puzzled
25. [A] pride [B] failure [C] regret [D] surprise
26. [A] doctor [B] store owner [C] bookseller [D] TV reporter
27. [A] pay [B] cost [C] afford [D] spend
28. [A] shame [B] honor [C] horror [D] danger
29. [A] advised [B] forced [C] persuaded [D] permitted
30. [A] action [B] program [C] treatment [D] operation
31. [A] repaired [B] connected [C] injured [D] improved
32. [A] pleasure [B] sadness [C] interest [D] disappointment
33. [A] at the TV station [B] in the Students Union
    [C] at the U.S. Forest Service [D] at McCarley's Bookstore
34. [A] so [B] and [C] but [D] because
35. [A] readers [B] viewers [C] customers [D] passengers

第三部分 阅读理解

阅读下列短文,从每题所给的四个选项([A]、[B]、[C]、[D])中选出最佳选项,并在答题卡上将该项涂黑。

A

Bamboo is one of the nature's most surprising plants. Many people call this plant a tree, but it is a kind of grass.

Like other kinds of grass, a bamboo plant may be cut very low to the ground, but it will grow back very quickly. A Japanese scientist recorded one bamboo plant that grew almost 1.5

meters in 24 hours! Bamboo grows almost everywhere in the world except Europe. There are more than 1,000 kinds of bamboo that grow around the world on both mountains and plains.

Not all bamboo looks the same. Some bamboo plants are very thin. They may only grow to be a few centimeters wide while others may grow to more than 30 centimeters across. This plant also comes in different colors, from yellow to black to green.

Many Asian countries have been using bamboo for hundreds of years. They often use bamboo for building new buildings. As a matter of fact, the cables (绳索) that hold up the hanging bridge across the Min River in Sichuan are made of bamboo. The bridge has been in use for more than 1,000 years, and is still holding strong.

In Africa, engineers are teaching poor farmers how to find water using bamboo. These African countries need cheap ways to find water because they have no money, and their fields often die from no rain and no water. It seems that bamboo is one of the best things they can use. Bamboo pipes and drills (钻) can help to make the poor thirsty fields to be watered.

36. How is bamboo like grass?
    [A] It is thin and easy to cut.   [B] It grows everywhere.
    [C] It grows quickly after it is cut short.   [D] It is short and green.
37. The sentence "while others may grow to more than 30 centimeters across." means "Some other bamboo plants may grow to be very _____."
    [A] short   [B] strong   [C] thick   [D] tall
38. From the text we know _____.
    [A] most people call bamboo plant trees
    [B] a bamboo plant may grow 4.5 meters in three days
    [C] the bamboo plant changes its colors when it grows
    [D] a bridge held by bamboo cable was built thousands of years ago
39. Why did the engineers teach the poor farmers in Africa to make use of bamboo?
    [A] Because it is cheap.   [B] Because it is colorful.
    [C] Because it drills fast.   [D] Because it is used by Asians.
40. Which of the following is NOT true?
    [A] There are many different kinds of bamboo with different colors.
    [B] Cables made of bamboo can last for over a thousand years.
    [C] Bamboo can be used for buildings, bridges and watering projects (工程).
    [D] Bamboo plants are able to grow well in any part of the world.

B

Do you know Australia? Australia is the largest island in the world. It is a little smaller than China. It is in the south of the earth. Australia is big, but its population is not large. The population of Australia is nearly as large as that of Shanghai.

The government has made enough laws to fight pollution. The cities in Australia have got little air or water pollution. The sky is blue and the water is clean. You can clearly see fish swimming in the rivers. Plants grow very well.

Last month (Now it is August) we visited Perth, the biggest city in Western Australia, and went to a wild flowers' exhibition. There we saw a large number of wild flowers we had never seen before. We had a wonderful time. Perth is famous for its beautiful wild flowers. In spring every year Perth has the wild flowers' exhibition. After visiting Perth, we spent the day in the countryside. We sat down and had a rest near a path at the foot of a hill. It was quiet and we enjoyed ourselves. Suddenly we heard bells ringing at the top of the hill. What we saw made us pick up all our things and run back to the car as quickly as we could. There were about three hundred sheep coming towards us down the path.

Australia is famous for its sheep and kangaroos (袋鼠). After a short drive from any town, you will find yourself in the middle of white sheep. Sheep, sheep, everywhere are sheep.

41. Australia is _____.
    [A] the largest country in the world
    [B] as large as Shanghai
    [C] not as large as China
    [D] the largest island in the north of the earth

42. The government had made _____.
    [A] too enough laws to fight pollution
    [B] so many laws that it can fight pollution
    [C] enough laws that it can hardly fight pollution
    [D] enough laws because the pollution is very serious

43. Which of the following is NOT true?
    [A] Perth is famous for its beautiful wild flowers.
    [B] Perth is bigger than any other city in Western Australia.
    [C] Perth lies in the west of Australia.
    [D] No other city is larger than Perth in Australia.

44. In Perth you may visit a wild flowers' show in _____.
    [A] October   [B] January   [C] May   [D] July

45. Which of the following is true?
    [A] Australia is famous for its sheep, kangaroos and wild flowers.
    [B] We ran back to the car because we were in the middle of white sheep.
    [C] Three hundred sheep came towards us because they saw us.
    [D] If you go to the countryside in Australia, you will see a large number of white sheep.

C

The history of the Games

Olympia

Olympia, the site of the ancient Olympic Games, is in the western part of the Peloponnese which, according to Greek mythology, is the island of "Pelops", the founder of the Olympic Games. Imposing temples, votive buildings, elaborate shrines and ancient sporting facilities (设备) were combined in a site of unique natural and mystical beauty.

Olympia functioned as a meeting place for worship and other religious and political practices as early as the 10th century B. C. The central part of Olympia was dominated by the majestic temple of Zeus, with the temple of Hera parallel to it. The ancient stadium in Olympia could hold more than 40,000 audience, while in the surrounding area there were auxiliary (辅助的) buildings which developed gradually up until the 4th century B. C. and were used as training sites for the athletes or to house the judges of the Games.

The Games and Religion

The Olympic Games were closely linked to the religious festivals of the cult of Zeus, but were not a total part of a rite. Indeed, they had a secular character and aimed to show the physical qualities and development of the performances accomplished by young people, as well as encouraging good relations between the cities of Greece. According to specialists, the Olympic Games owed their purity and importance to religion.

Victory Ceremonies

The Olympic victor received his first awards immediately after the competition. Following the announcement of the winner's name by the herald, a Hellanodikis (Greek judge) would place a palm branch in his hands, while the audience cheered and threw flowers to him. Red ribbons were tied on his head and hands as a mark of victory.

The official award ceremony would take place on the last day of the Games, at the elevated vestibule of the temple of Zeus. In a loud voice, the herald would announce the name of the Olympic winner, his father's name, and his homeland. Then, the Hellanodikis placed the sacred olive tree wreath, or Kotinos, on the winner's head.

46. When did Olympia become the site of the Olympic Games?

　　[A] In the 10th century B. C.　　　　[B] Before the 4th century B. C.

　　[C] After the 4th century B. C.　　　　[D] It was not mentioned here.

47. Which one is TRUE according to the passage?

　　[A] Zeus is the founder of the Olympic Games.

　　[B] The ancient stadium in Olympic were used as training sites for the athletes in the 10th century.

　　[C] The Olympic Games have much to do with the religion.

　　[D] The Olympic victor would receive a golden medal.

48. Can you guess the meaning of this word "herald" in the passage?

　　[A] Author.　　　　[B] Headmaster.　　　　[C] Announcer.　　　　[D] Manager.

49. When the athletes won the game, _____.

　　[A] They were awarded immediately after the competition

　　[B] They were awarded twice. The first, immediately after the competition; the second, on the last day of the game

[C] They were awarded on the last day of the game
[D] They were awarded on the last day of the game or immediately after the competition

D

Most people, when they travel to space, would like to stay in orbit for a few days of more. And this stands to reason, if you're paying $20,000 for your trip to orbit! Strain order for tourism to reach its full potential there's going to be a need for orbital accommodation—or space hotels. What would a space hotel actually be like to visit? Hotels in orbit will offer the services you expect from a hotel—private rooms, meals and bars. But they'll also offer two unique experiences: impressive views—of Earth and space—and the endless entertainment of living in zero gravity—including sports and other activities that make use of this.

The hotels themselves will vary greatly—from being quite simple in the early days to huge luxury structure at a later date. It's actually surprising that as later as 1997, very few designs for space hotels were published. This is mainly because those who might be expected to design them haven't expected launch costs to come down far enough to make them possible.

Lots of people who've been to space have described vividly what it's like to live in zero gravity. There are obviously all sorts of possibilities for dancing, gymnastics, and zero-G sports. Luckily, you don't need to sleep much living in zero gravity, so you'll have plenty of time for relaxing by hanging out in a bar with a window looking down at the turning Earth below.

Of course all good things have come to an end. Unfortunately, and so after a few days you'll find yourself heading back enough you'll be much more expert at exercising in zero gravity than you were when you arrived. You'll be thinking how soon you can save up enough to get back up again—or maybe you should change jobs to get to work in an orbiting hotel.

50. When traveling in space, most people would like to stay in orbit for a few days because _____.

[A] it is expensive to travel in space
[B] they would find the possible life in other star systems
[C] they could enjoy the luxury of space hotels
[D] they want to realize the full potential of tourism

51. Which of the following is NOT discussed in the passage?

[A] When was the space traveling made possible.
[B] What are the unique experiences that space hotels will offer.
[C] Why were there not many published designs for space hotels.
[D] How can the travelers enjoy themselves in space hotels.

52. This passage is mainly about _____.

[A] traveling in space
[B] the ways of living in space hotels
[C] zero gravity and space hotels
[D] the description of space hotels

E

Dear Hamilton,

We are fortunate that in such a large, high-pressure office we all get along so well. You are one of the people who keep the social temperature at such a comfortable setting. I don't know anyone in the office who is better liked than you.

You can perhaps help with this. The collection of <u>contributions</u> towards gifts for employees' personal-life events is becoming a little troubling. Certainly, the group sending of a gift is reasonable now and then. In the past month, however, there have been collections for two baby shower gifts, one wedding shower gift, two wedding gifts, one funeral（葬礼）remembrance, four birthday gifts, and three graduation gifts.

It's not only the collected—from who are growing uncomfortable (and poor), but the collected—for feel uneasy receiving gifts from people who don't know them outside the office, who wouldn't even recognize their graduating children, their marrying daughters and sons, or their dead relatives.

This is basically a kind gesture (and one that people think well of you for), but the practice seems to have become too wide-ranging and feels improper in today's office setting.

Thank you for understanding.

53. The underlined word "contributions" probably means _____.

　　[A] money　　　　[B] suggestions　　　　[C] reports　　　　[D] understanding

54. Hamilton is expected to _____.

　　[A] show more kindness

　　[B] discontinue the present practice

　　[C] quit being the organizer for gift giving

　　[D] know more about co-workers' families

55. This is basically a letter of _____.

　　[A] apology　　　　[B] sympathy　　　　[C] appreciation　　　　[D] dissatisfaction

第四部分　写　　作

第一节　短文改错

此题要求改正所给短文中的错误。对标有题号的每一行做出判断：如无错误，在该行右边横线上画一个勾（√）；如有错误（每行只有一个错误），则按下列情况改正：

此行多一个词：把多余的词用斜线（\）划掉，在该行右边横线上写出该词，并也用斜线划掉。

此行缺一个词：在缺词处加一个漏字符号（∧），在该行右边横线上写出该加的词。

此行错一个词：在错的词下画一横线，在该行右边横线上写出改正后的词。

注意：原行没有错的不要改。

Most smokers want to stop smoke. Many of　　　　56. _____
them have tried more than once but failed.　　　　57. _____
Although they know smoking may kill them and　　58. _____
cause a serious illness yet they can give it up.　　　59. _____
The reason to it is that tobacco contains nicotine　　60. _____
that is a drug which gets one into habit of smoking.　61. _____
Because you start taking the drug, it is hard to stop.　62. _____
If you go without it for an hour or two, it　　　　63. _____
begin to feel bad. The only thing can stop　　　　64. _____
you feeling bad is the drug containing in your body.　65. _____

第二节　书面表达

假定你是李明。英语报正在对"快餐在中国的流行"进行讨论，请写一封短信，谈谈你对快餐的一些看法和建议。

要点如下：

1. 快餐流行的原因；
2. 个人对快餐的看法；
3. 提出建议。

注意：词数 100 个左右。

参考答案及解析

第一部分　单项填空

1. D【解析】本题考查冠词。第一个空是说话双方都知道的事物，用定冠词。a minute "一分钟，一会儿"，是泛指，不确定的。

2. D【解析】本题考查定语从句。先行词 the one 在从句中作地点状语，用关系副词 where。

3. A【解析】本题考查名词性从句。_____ is now a famous holiday center 部分作 in 的介词宾语从句，而宾语从句中又缺少主语，要用 what，意为 a place that/which。

4. D【解析】本题考查副词。根据 not a minute early or late. 可以推出是"按时、准时"。flexibly 意为"灵活地"；temporarily 意为"暂时地；临时的"；approximately 意为"大约地"。

5. D【解析】本题考查定语从句。先行词 other activities 在定语从句中作 you can meet people 抽象的地点状语，用关系副词。

6. C【解析】本题考查连词。根据句子含义，构成了 not...but 结构，nor the way they appear to be 的出现，增加了题目的迷惑性。

7. A【解析】本题考查代词，空格上要填的词作 students 的同位语，两者都是 has 的宾语，要用宾格。

8. C【解析】本题考查主谓一致。句子的主语是 the time，是第三人称单数；并且根据句子的时态，要选一般现在时。

9. B【解析】Take it easy＝not to work too hard "慢慢来；别着忙"；Take your time（over）＝ to use as much time as is necessary; not hurry. Do as you like "你怎么喜欢怎么做"。

10. A【解析】本句想说明：经济发展是一种双赢或多赢的游戏，can 此处为情态动词表"能够"或"有时候会"之意。

11. A【解析】本句考查强调结构的省略用法，补全后为：It was only some of them that were carried to their kindergarten.

12. A【解析】本句最重要的标志符号为第二句中的逗号：前后如为主句和从句之间关系，必有连词；既然没有连词，且后一句为完整句，前半部分势必为独立主格结构。排除 C 项；B、D 分别因时态和语态不正确排除。

13. C【解析】本句考查状语提前后，句子的语序问题。如状语提前，且句子主语不为人称代词，此时句子主语、谓语完全倒装，类似于 in the front hangs a portrait.

14. B【解析】本题考查词义辨析：take care of 意为"照顾（尤其指病人）"；take into account 意为"考虑"，相当于 take into consideration, take notice of 意为"有意，注意"；put up with 意为"容忍"，类似于 tolerate。本句意为：我得先考虑他在生意圈的信誉，然后决定是否批准贷款给他。

15. C【解析】Can't complain 也作 I can't complain，意思为"没说的"，表示对事情的满意。B 项中 cross one's fingers＝hope that one's plan will be successful "祈求成功"。Keep your fingers crossed！"祈求好运吧！"

第二部分　完形填空

16. B【解析】当你到书店的书架前，你首先看到的是书的"名称/题目"。

17. C【解析】柜台后面一般是售货员或店老板，因为选项中没有售货员，因此答案是"店老板"。

18. B【解析】根据下文作者的回答可知老板问作者是否想找"一份工作"。

19. B【解析】因为上大学需要钱，所以需要"积攒，节省"。

20. D【解析】根据上文"找工作"可得出答案。

21. C【解析】根据下文，尤其是"I felt in having helped her"这句话可以猜出答案。

22. D【解析】根据下文和本句中的副词 almost（我几乎把书店里所有的书都给她看了）可得出答案。

23. D【解析】文章开头第一句就交代了"书店"，上下文都可以证实。

24. A【解析】根据上文作者的热情服务把书店几乎所有的书都拿给她看，以及下文作者对自己工作的满意心情可以判断，那位妇女走时是带着"不太着急的"心情离开的。

25. A【解析】从上文的叙述和下文的"I felt in having helped her"可知作者因帮助了这样一位妇女而感到很"自豪"。

26. D【解析】根据下文的 NBC News 得出答案是电视台记者。

27. C【解析】因为是移民，因此判断他家里"付不起"矫正的手术费。

28. A【解析】因为手是残疾，再根据后面"把手藏在口袋里"判断答案为"害羞"。

29. C【解析】根据下文"我写的故事被播出了"可知我"说服"了老板让我写这个故事。

30. D【解析】从上文提到"矫正手术"得出答案。

31. A【解析】从上文，手术后在医院康复期间，作者看望了那个小孩，他做的第一件事就是举起他那动手术"修复过"的手。

32. A【解析】看到那个小孩举起他的手，我有一种"高兴"的感觉。

33. D【解析】从文章的第一句话可得出答案。
34. C【解析】从句子的前后意思可知表示转折关系。
35. B【解析】因为作者现在是一位电视工作者，所做的工作是为"看电视的观众"而做的。

第三部分 阅读理解

A

36. C【解析】由第二段的第一句我们可以推测出竹子与其他草类相似的地方是 grow back very quickly。
37. C【解析】阅读第三段的第二句"They may only grow to be a few centimeters wide while others may grow to more than 30 centimeters across"可推知：while（表对比，意为"而"）前面讲有些竹子（bamboo）很细，只有（only）几厘米粗，而与其相比，while 后面则讲有些竹子长得很壮，可以有 30 厘米粗。因此答案选 C。
38. B【解析】由第二段我们可知竹子一天能长 1.5 米，那么三天就能长 4.5 米。
39. A【解析】根据第五段第二句"Because they have no money"可知要选用 bamboo。
40. D【解析】第二段的倒数第二句中说 except Europe，由此可知答案为 D。

B

41. C【解析】细节题。根据第一段的第二、三句"Australia is the largest island in the world. It is a little smaller than China"可知答案选 C。
42. B【解析】细节题。根据第二段的"The government has made enough laws to fight pollution"可知答案选 B。
43. D【解析】由第三段的第一句"the biggest city in..."我们可以推测出 Perth 是澳大利亚西部最大的城市，而选项 D 则说它是澳大利亚最大的城市，所以答案选 D。
44. D【解析】根据第三段中的"Last month we visited Perth, the biggest city in Western Australia..."答案选 D。
45. D【解析】从最后一段的"After a short drive from any town, you will find yourself in the middle of white sheep..."可以判断出答案选 D。

C

46. B【解析】文章第二段提到公元前四世纪的时候奥林匹亚运动场建造的辅助设施用来训练运动员或裁判员休息，可见那时已经开始举行奥运会了。
47. C【解析】文章第三段说到奥运会与宗教有很大的关系。
48. C【解析】从文章后两段可以看出，"herald"是宣布获奖结果的，所以可以推测出应当是宣告员。
49. B【解析】文章倒数第二段提到第一次颁奖是在比赛结束时立即进行，最后一段又提到了官方的奖励，可见是有两次颁奖。

D

50. A【解析】推理判断题。从第一段第一、二句"Most people, when they travel to space, would like to stay in orbit for a few days of more. And this stands to reason, if you're paying $20,000 for your trip to orbit!"和文章最后一段最后一句可推断出太空旅行因为价格昂贵目前只是少数人才能实现，但是这一切都是值得的，没有理由来了一次不去住 space

hotels。

51. A【解析】推理判断题。只有 A 项从未提及，B 项在第一段最后一句提到过，C 项在第二段可以找到依据，D 项则在第三段进行了详细的介绍。

52. D【解析】主旨大意题。从全文不难得出文章主要介绍了太空旅馆的情况。A 项范围太广，B 项以偏概全，C 项不恰当并非介绍两者之间的关系。

E

53. A【解析】第二段说明，收取各种礼物的费用，所以 contributions 指 money。

54. B【解析】考查理解深层含义的能力。这封信向 Hamilton 说明了一些收取礼物费用的好处和带来的一些麻烦，请求他能够理解，所以推断他可能不会进行这种习俗了。

55. D【解析】考查理解深层含义的能力。这封信对 Hamilton 说明了一些收取礼物费用的好处和带来的一些麻烦，请求他能够理解，所以推断他可能不会进行这种习俗了。文中最后还说明，虽然这是一慈善的举动，但想说服 Hamilton 中断这种交钱买礼物的习俗。从写信人的语气中可以看出，这是一封表示不满情绪的信。

第四部分 写 作

第一节 短文改错

56. smoke →smoking
57. √
58. and→or
59. can→can't/can not
60. to→for（of）
61. habit 前面加 the
62. Because→Once/If
63. 第二个 it→you
64. thing 后加 that
65. containing→contained

第二节 书面表达

Fast Food

Fast food is becoming more and more popular in China, especially among children. There are several reasons for its popularity.

First, it is very convenient and saves a lot of time. You just go into a fast food restaurant, order your food, and your food is ready immediately. You can either eat it there or take it away. Second, it is very clean and comfortable and it has the excellent service and good quality of food.

However, fast food is far from satisfactory. Eating more fast food is not good to our health. Thus, doctors suggest that people, especially children, eat fast food as little as possible. Although cooking at home needs more time, it offers healthy and delicious meals your body needs.

Key to Test Paper 2

Part I Listening Comprehension

Section A

1. B   2. C   3. A   4. C   5. B

Typescript

Directions: This section is to test your ability to understand short dialogue. There are 5 recorded dialogues in it. After each dialogue, there is a recorded question. The dialogues and questions will be spoken two times. When you hear a question, you should decide on the correct answer from the 4 choices marked A), B), C) and D) given in your test paper. Then you should mark the corresponding letter on the Answer Sheet with a single line through the centre.

1. W: When are you leaving for Cambridge, Dr. Berle?
   M: On Wednesday, that's tomorrow.
   Q: What day is today?
2. M: Shall we go to the cinema after dinner, Jane?
   W: I'd love to, but I have a report to write.
   Q: What does the woman mean?
3. W: May I speak to David Jefferson?
   M: I'm sorry, nobody by that name works here.
   Q: What do we learn from the conversation?
4. M: Excuse me, could you tell me if there's a bank near this post office?
   W: Well, there's one next to the supermarket, just to the right of the entrance.
   Q: Where is the bank?
5. W: Attention, please. Professor Smith wants us to hand in a paper on psychology by Monday morning.
   M: Another paper for him? My goodness. We did one only last week.
   Q: What's the man's reaction to the announcement?

Section B

6. B   7. C   8. A   9. D   10. B

Typescript

Directions: This section is to test your ability to understand short conversations. There are 2 recorded conversations in it. After each conversation, there are recorded questions. The conversations and questions will be spoken two times. When you hear a question, you should decide on the correct answer from the 4 choices marked A), B), C) and D) given in your test paper. Then you should mark the corresponding letter on the Answer Sheet with a single line through the centre.

Unit 8

Conversation 1

M: Helen, can I have a look at your newspaper?

W: Sure, go ahead.

M: I want to know what's on this weekend.

W: Is there anything interesting?

M: The Red Roses are giving a performance today.

W: They are a pop group. They are said to be very good. What time does the performance start?

M: 7 pm. Will you be free then?

W: Yes, I'd like to go.

M: Let's go together then.

W: All right.

Questions 6 and 7 are based on the conversation you've just heard.

6. What does the Red Roses refer to?

7. What have the two speakers decided to do?

Conversation 2

W: Hello, Air Traveler. What can I do for you, Sir?

M: Can I book a ticket to New York for next Friday, please?

W: Sure, but all the tickets of direct flights from Beijing are sold out. Would you mind a transfer ticket?

M: No. Where shall I go first, Hong Kong or Tokyo?

W: Tokyo. You'll wait there only for a couple of hours.

M: Well, that doesn't sound too bad. When can I get the ticket?

W: Any time. Would you like to have it delivered to you?

M: Yes, please.

W: Ok. But you've got to pay in cash rather than use your credit card.

M: No problem. Can I have a discount?

W: Yes, a ten percent discount.

M: Fine, thanks.

Questions 8 to 10 are based on the conversation you've just heard.

8. Where will the man transfer his flight?

9. How will the man get the ticket?

10. What's the discount allowed?

Section C

11. two weeks   12. the airport   13. dirty   14. mountains   15. a whole day

Typescript

Directions: This section is to test your ability to understand short passages. There is one recorded passage. After the passage, there will be 5 questions. The passage and questions will be spoken two times. When you hear a question, you should decide on the correct answer from the 4 choices marked A), B), C) and D) given in your test paper. Then you should mark the corresponding letter on the Answer Sheet with a single line through the centre.

Last Christmas I went to Hollywood for two weeks. My best friend was living there. I travelled by plane to Los Angeles, which took 13 hours. My friend picked me up at the airport and drove me in her car back to Hollywood. At first I was rather disappointed at the city because it looked rather dirty. However, after I'd recovered from the flight, my friend started taking me to see some wonderful sights. She lived in a beautiful house up in the mountains. The place was very beautiful and seemed like a part of another city. She drove me through all the expensive areas where the houses are absolutely enormous. We went to Disneyland and spent a whole day there. I didn't think I would enjoy it very much, but I did.

Questions 11 to 15 are based on the passage you've just heard.
11. How long did the speaker stay in Hollywood last Christmas?
12. Where did the speaker meet his best friend?
13. Why was the speaker disappointed when they drove to Hollywood?
14. Where was the speaker's friend's house?
15. How much time did they spend in Disneyland?

Part II Vocabulary & Structure
Section A
16. A   17. B   18. C   19. D   20. C
21. C   22. D   23. C   24. D   25. B
Section B
26. exciting   27. to type   28. musician   29. had known   30. hard-working
31. practical 32. coming   33. misunderstanding 34. to attend   35. was cheating (cheated)

Part III Reading Comprehension
Task 1
36. D   37. B   38. C   39. D   40. C
Task 2
41. B   42. A   43. B   44. C   45. B
Task 3
46. IT Page   47. every Sunday   48. technological breakthroughs
49. latest developments   50. IT companies
Task 4
51. L   52. G   53. C   54. N   55. H
Task 5
56. Packaging machinery   57. Chicago, Illinois   58. 2000
59. The leading role   60. a company/companies

Part IV Translation—English to Chinese

61. C   62. A   63. A   64. D

65. 参考译文：我外出几天，今天上午回到办公室，见到你10月1日写给我的邀请信，深表感谢。我非常希望能接受你的邀请，但不巧与几个海外朋友有约在先，不能如愿，深表歉意。

Part V Writing

参考范文：

Dear Sir or Madam,

  I am writing this letter to complain about a camera, which I bought in your shop last month when I was in Guangzhou on business. I took some pictures there with it. But when I got home and had the film developed, I found no pictures printed at all. I am very upset about it. I have already sent the camera back to you by post and strongly insist that you refund me as soon as possible.

Yours faithfully,
Wang Lan